CHRISTIAN CONVERSION
AND MISSION

The American Society of Missiology Book Series provides a platform for those engaged in the praxis of mission. Theologians, social scientists, historians, mission executives, missionaries, and activists from diverse religious traditions and cultures come together to form the American Society of Missiology. They reflect deeply on matters related to what can be discerned as God's redeeming activity in the world. This Series amplifies their voices for the renewal of the church, the transformation of the world, and the glory of God.

American Society of Missiology Series, No. 68

CHRISTIAN CONVERSION AND MISSION

A Brief Cultural History

Andrew F. Walls

Mark R. Gornik, editor

ORBIS BOOKS
Maryknoll, New York 10545

Founded in 1970, Orbis Books endeavors to publish works that enlighten the mind, nourish the spirit, and challenge the conscience. The publishing arm of the Maryknoll Fathers and Brothers, Orbis seeks to explore the global dimensions of the Christian faith and mission, to invite dialogue with diverse cultures and religious traditions, and to serve the cause of reconciliation and peace. The books published reflect the views of their authors and do not represent the official position of the Maryknoll Society. To learn more about Maryknoll and Orbis Books, please visit our website at www.orbisbooks.com.

Copyright © 2025 by © Ingrid Walls

Published by Orbis Books, Box 302, Maryknoll, NY 10545-0302.

Manufactured in the United States of America

Library of Congress Cataloging-in-Publication Data

Names: Walls, Andrew F. (Andrew Finlay), author. | Gornik, Mark R., editor.
Title: Christian conversion and mission : a brief cultural history / Andrew F. Walls ; Mark R. Gornik, editor.
Description: Maryknoll, NY : Orbis Books, [2025] | Series: American society of missiology; 68 | Includes bibliographical references and index. | Summary: "Traces the theme of conversion throughout the history of Christian missionary expansion"— Provided by publisher.
Identifiers: LCCN 2024044316 (print) | LCCN 2024044317 (ebook) | ISBN 9781626986176 (trade paperback) | ISBN 9798888660720 (epub)
Subjects: LCSH: Conversion—Christianity—History. | Missions—History.
Classification: LCC BV4916 .W33 2025 (print) | LCC BV4916 (ebook) | DDC 248.2/409—dc23/eng/20241125
LC record available at https://lccn.loc.gov/2024044316
LC ebook record available at https://lccn.loc.gov/2024044317

To Bill Burrows

and

Akrofi-Christaller Institute
of Theology, Mission and Culture

Contents

Epilogue

Preface to the American Society of Missiology Series

Beyond the bare-bones definition of missiology as the study of the church's worldwide mission, missiology explores the intersection of active faith and culture. As such, it is well positioned to provide invaluable resources for those who seek to understand the interaction between God, the engaged church, and the cultures of the world. The American Society of Missiology Book Series seeks to publish these resources and make them available for the wider church.

Missiology is interdisciplinary, intercultural, and international. Theologians, social scientists, historians, linguists, and other specialized disciplines have come together to form the American Society of Missiology (ASM). These scholars, who hail from their respective traditions and rich cultures, reflect on matters related to what can be discerned as God's redeeming activity in the world. This series amplifies their voices for the renewal of the church, the transformation of the world, and the glory of God.

Missiology can also be described as praxiological—that is, it is at once theoretical and practical. It was the Brazilian educator Paulo Freire who defined "praxis" as "action and reflection upon the world in order to transform it." Missiology is scholarship in the service of the church-in-mission, and vice versa: the practice of the church in the world serves missiological scholarship like nothing else can. Many mission executives, missionaries, and activists also belong to the society. ASM is a rich community of scholar-practitioners who seek to make a contribution not only to the scholarly field of mission studies but also to the "trenches" where gospel bearers give of their blood, sweat, and tears for the sake of mission.

In collaboration with Orbis Books, whose commitment to praxis is core to its mission, the ASM Book Series seeks to make available relevant resources for both scholars and practitioners of *missio Dei.* We welcome your engagement and feedback; and should you feel inspired to contribute to this series, we also welcome your submissions.

Al Tizon, ASM Series Editor
Darrell Whiteman, ASM Publisher

Introduction

Turn, Turn

Conversion is about turning toward Christ
what is already there.

—Andrew Walls

For more than forty years, Andrew Walls sustained a project—in thinking, writing, and speaking—that mattered perhaps more to him than any other: a cultural history of Christian conversion, which is to say, a cultural history of Christ's mission and the life of the gospel. As Walls, who died in 2021 at the age of ninety-three, envisioned it, this work would take "account of the variety of geographical, historical and cultural settings in which conversion has appeared over the two millennia of Christian presence." No small project, he recognized, and he kept at this reflection on Christian faith.

The very idea of conversion, a term that can bring to mind images of coercion and imposed cultural change, often evokes significant concern, and rightly so. But what Walls had to say about Christian conversion and its meaning for everyday life and thought is far more interesting than we may have imagined, and very different from common perceptions.

For Walls, Christian conversion is a continual process of turning, and so to study conversion requires a consideration of who is turning, and from where and when they turn. Conversion is turning toward Christ as persons and communities, and toward Christ from within a particular culture, place, and time. It is turning by the Spirit, who guides the risky work of faith that involves learning and listening, in the deep engagement with culture that conversion entails.

This idea of turning toward, not away, Walls found, and as his wife Ingrid Walls has recalled, is best captured in the Shaker song "Simple Gifts," and the last two lines in particular:

> 'Tis the gift to be simple, 'tis the gift to be free,
> 'Tis the gift to come down where we ought to be,
> And when we find ourselves in the place just right,
> 'Twill be in the valley of love and delight.
> When true simplicity is gain'd,
> To bow and to bend we will not be asham'd,
> To turn, turn will be our delight,
> Till by turning, turning we come round right.

Underlined by virtues of simplicity and fittingness, "Simple Gifts" finds "turning" from within a "turning" until we "come round right." In this dance of turning, turning, Walls also thought it was important that the mirror of Christ be turned toward culture, to "come round right." If this is also a Shaker dance song, even more apt for a Scot!

Andrew Walls did not see his book on conversion come to completion; there were chapters still very much in mind at the time of his death. But in lectures, essays, and unpublished notes, he left the contours and markers of this project. As best as possible, based on discussions with Walls over the years on the chapters and themes of his projected work, this volume has sought to gather these "patches" of words and ideas from across the years that yet render a whole.

These collected works are organized into two main sections: Lectures and Encounters. These sections open with a prologue, which comprises material drawn from Walls's formative essay "Converts of Proselytes? The Crisis over the Conversion in the Early Church" and the opening lecture of the chapters that follow. It was important to Walls, in his project of completing a cultural history of conversion, to engage with the Church's earliest considerations of Christ and conversion.

The four chapters in the first section are unpublished transcripts from lectures that Walls delivered at Fuller Theological Seminary in 1996 under the title "A Cultural History of the Christian Faith: Eusebius Revisited and Latourette Reconsidered." These lectures were the basis for a 1997 symposium held at the Center for Mission Study and Research at Maryknoll, in New York. It was at this symposium that Bill Burrows, Walls's friend and Orbis Books editor, expressed his belief that the "conversion book" was groundbreaking, and ready to be published as is. Walls felt there was more to do, however, and continued to deliver versions of these lectures in a myriad of settings, ever refining his material. The lectures are now published here as a whole, with a few words edited for clarity.

The people and places in these lectures were Walls's companions across his lifetime of work—among them Antony, Origen, Justin, St. Patrick, Bede, Africa, Asia, Latin America, and Europe. For Walls, the scriptural narrative, especially as found in the Acts of the Apostles, was critical for his understanding of conversion and its concurring themes, such as translation, change, and community. This framework is continually referenced by Walls as he develops his understanding not just of conversion but Christian faith and mission,

Following the lecture series are three chapters that Walls wrote to deepen and elaborate his argument about Christian conversion, faith, and mission. The first, "Worldviews and Christian Conversion," seeks to convey some of the implications that he saw for theology, thought, and life. The second, "Monks and Evangelicals"—drawn from unpublished lecture transcripts now found in *The Missionary Movement from the West: A Biography from Birth to Old Age*—was intended to be a fuller chapter in his book on conversion. The third, "When World Christianity Fell Apart," which involves a reading of early church life and the meaning of its decisions, was envisioned both as a chapter in this cultural history of conversion as well as part of Walls' wider study of early Christianity.

The epilogue is "Conversion and Christian Continuity," an essay from 1980 that Walls described as "incorporating material" from his earlier and noted essay "Culture and Coherence in Christian History," which was published in his first Orbis volume, *The Missionary Movement in Christian History: Studies in the Transmission of Faith*. It is a summary, not a full historical presentation, around Christian faith and culture as he would develop further. Notable, however, in the version of the essay included here, is its conclusion. Rather than end, as in the earlier essay, with an invitation to consider who Christian believers are called to be to one another, here Walls concludes by emphasizing that conversion involves that dance of turning, turning over generations.

Looking to the future of Christianity is a fitting way not only to bring this project to a conclusion, but to honor the legacy and work that Walls hands along to historians, scholars, and perhaps most of all, congregations of faith and communities in mission calling. As Walls emphasized, the difference between being a convert or a proselyte remains a very real concern for the world Christian community.

This book would not be possible without a community of friends and fellow travelers of Andrew Walls. Bill Burrows, formerly managing editor of Orbis Books, not only saw the work of Andrew Walls into print but had the vision to bring to publication the conversion lectures that are found here. Stephanie Conning with the Maryknoll Mission Archives provided a copy of the lectures that are published here and that served as a basis for the symposium held in 1997 at Maryknoll. And for these lectures, we recall the role of the late Wilbert Shenk at Fuller Theological Seminary in also bringing this material forward.

Much honor is due to Robert Ellsberg, publisher of Orbis Books, who has long kept faith with this project and has now seen it into print, providing a seasoned editor's critical engagement with the work at hand.

Hannah Newman-Pan, City Seminary of New York colleague, did much to help this project and shared an enthusiasm for seeing this come together. Christy Choi and Juliya Joseph joined in for close reading and bibliographic work. Afia Sun Kim and Sarah Gerth van den Berg gave this work an important read in its final stages.. And City Seminary of New York has held this work close in prayer and with the support that matters to such a project.

The entire community of Akrofi-Christaller Institute of Theology, Mission and Culture in Ghana; Brian Stanley and the Centre for the Study of World Christianity at the University of Edinburgh; and Abraham Ng'ang'a and the Andrew F. Walls Centre for the Study of African and Asian Christianity at Liverpool Hope University were institutional settings for the work Walls sought to do as is represented here.

Ingrid Walls has been essential to every stage of this project, and this book would not be here without her commitment and encouragement; it is also a journey that she shares with the late Doreen Walls, and does so with gratitude and honor for her life. To think about the story of this book is to also recognize the enduring love of Christine, Alan, Andrew, Fengyu, and Alice.

Finally, thank you, Andrew Walls, for keeping at this project across the years, not least because the ongoing call of God to conversion remains an urgent matter of faith for our times.

Mark R. Gornik

Prologue

I realize now that the title of this set of lectures, "A Cultural History of the Christian Faith: Eusebius Revisited and Latourette Reconsidered," is absurdly presumptuous. It invokes the name of both the father of church history and of the most comprehensive and encyclopedic historian of the Christian faith to date and may imply some pontifical reassessment of their work. Let me make clear from the outset that such is not my intention. Valuable as it might be to consider how either or both engage with the material of Christian history that was known to them, my immediate concern is merely the example they set—one in the fourth and one in the twentieth century—of attempting to review Christian history as a whole. I wish to revisit their subject matter rather than the historiography, to reconsider their theme rather than their execution of it.

Each of them wrote at a period which each recognized as epochal. Eusebius realized that with Constantine's abandonment of the state struggle against Christianity, a new chapter of Christian experience was opening, and as he celebrated the martyrs whose endurance had made it possible, he gave thanks that Caesar himself was about to render tribute of the things that were God's. Latourette wrote as the Second World War brought to a climax a period that had begun with the First and had brought to an end what he saw as the great century of Christian expansion of the nineteenth century. He who characterized

1

Christian history by its periods of advance and recession was unsure, seeing signs of both in the period since 1914, though he was willing to believe that those of advance might preponderate in this, the latest Christian age.

We may now applaud his prescience, for the latest stage has been marked by both advance and recession, one that has turned the conceptions of the great century upside down, for the advance has taken place in Africa and Asia and in a special form in Latin America, the recession in the Western countries. Every year Christianity becomes more and more emphatically a non-Western religion, and that is perhaps its most outstanding feature as its third millennium begins. This fact may give added reason to emulate Eusebius and Latourette in seeking to traverse Christian history as a whole, for it draws attention to a recurrent feature of that history, the serial nature of Christian expansion.

Christian history has not been the steady, triumphant, world-conquering process that Eusebius may be forgiven for expecting. It's been a serial process in which it has encountered successive cultures and found expression within them, often withering in the areas of its apparently greater strength and finding new homes in quite different soil. This feature suggests that there may be merit in a cultural history of Christianity, a retelling of the story in terms of Christian interaction with successive cultures, picking up a hint in the Epistle to the Ephesians that all are necessary to the full-grown humanity that will one day be revealed in Christ.

I must admit that when I learned of the great honor I was receiving in being invited to give these lectures and to use them as a reflection on the Latourette model, my heart leaped at the opportunity to do just such a cultural history, and I rashly proposed the present title. The attempt to prepare it, however, has brought me down to earth, and the scale of what would be required has defeated me.

Eusebius had less than four centuries to consider and needed more than one book per century. And Latourette, who had nineteen and one-half, took seven large volumes. I do not possess Latourette's admirable economy of style. I'm therefore presenting only a fragment of a larger work, with some chapters in the cultural history of our faith. They are, I believe, however, crucial chapters in the story, chapters with indicative value for understanding our present situation.

I'd invite you to consider with me in particular two continuing aspects of these chapters. One is the theme of translation, the process by which a Christian understanding is developed in successive bodies of thought, life, and tradition. Lamin Sanneh has put us all in his debt by drawing attention to translatability as a determinative feature of Christian existence.

But behind all the translation of words lies a still greater act of translation, that of the Word made flesh, of divinity translated into humanity. When that fundamental translation took place, it did so in an utterly culture-specific form in terms of the language, customs, and traditions of first-century Jewish Palestine. The Word was made flesh and spoke Aramaic, no doubt with a Galilean accent. All authentic Christian manifestations since then are retranslations of that original in terms of the language, customs, traditions, and cultures of other types and other places.

The second theme to which I point is that of conversion. If translation is seen as the characteristically Christian way of understanding the divine saving activity toward humanity, conversion is the characteristic way of understanding the proper human response to that activity. In what follows, therefore, I invite you to reflect on what might be called the natural history of conversion and the various forms it has taken in various chapters of Christian history as our predecessors in faith have sought to realize what Christ meant in terms of the accumulated wisdom, traditions, and inheritance of their times.

The word *conversion* has been used in Christian history in a multitude of ways. There have been at least two broad streams of usage, each with many divisions. In one stream, conversion is spoken of essentially as an external act of religious change. In this usage Christian conversion refers to movement to the Christian faith, individually or collectively, on the part of people previously outside it. By extension, this usage can also indicate movement from one branch of Christian profession to another—from Catholic to Protestant, for instance, or vice versa.

In the second stream of usage, "conversion" denotes critical internal religious change in persons within the Christian community, and here the varieties of meaning raise complex issues. Sometimes "conversion" refers to subjective experience, sometimes to an assumed ontological change, sometimes to both. For centuries in the Latin West, the primary meaning of "conversion" was a person's response to vocation to the religious or monastic life, turning from the life of the world to God. In Protestant devotion it came to refer to an early stage of the pilgrimage of the soul awakened to God.

Catholics, Jansenists, mainstream Protestants, radical Protestants, Puritans, Pietists, and Arminian and Calvinist evangelicals developed differing maps of the processes of salvation and differing paradigms of "normal" Christian experience. These in turn led to different assessments of the nature and significance of conversion and of its relationship to regeneration, justification, and other elements in the salvific process.

They also raised the question whether conversion was always necessary where Christian nurture had been effective. New styles of evangelism, with new understandings of the saving process, that developed in the nineteenth and twentieth centuries complicated matters further. Whole new vocabularies of evangelism came into existence, and the word "conversion" had a place in all of them. Where the vital question is, "Are you saved?" or "Have you accepted Jesus into your heart?" "conversion" is likely to mean something rather different from what it means when the question is, "How long have you been at Sinai, and what is your law work?" as it might be in the older Scottish evangelicalism, or "Have you the form of godliness, and do you desire the power thereof?" which might be raised if an inquirer sought membership of an early Methodist society.

The Protestant missionary movement complicated the understanding of conversion still further. Missions aimed to bring into the Christian faith those who were outside it, but those who were most active in establishing missions were often evangelicals, who had a well-defined paradigm of "normal" Christian experience. The evangelical conversion they had experienced had taken them from the "nominal" Christianity professed throughout the society in which they had grown up to "real" Christianity issuing in a holy life. This process was typically marked by a period of deep consciousness of personal sin followed by a sense of joyous liberation dawning with realization of personal forgiveness through Christ.

Missionaries with this background expected to see a similar pattern of experience in those who came to Christian faith, even in societies where there had been no previous Christian profession. In this way, the distinction between the two streams of usage—the one relating to externally recognizable adhesion to the Christian faith and the other relating to internal personal change—became blurred. This was not the first time that such blurring occurred. There had long been confusion within the first stream of usage when referring to such celebrated conversions as those of Constantine and Augustine, where "conversion" might be used equally of their identification (in their different ways) with the Christian community, or of the particular critical experiences that led them to it.

I do not attempt here to disentangle these linguistic and conceptual complexities. Instead, I shall focus on the simplest, most elemental feature of the word "conversion," the idea of turning. There is ample biblical warrant for this focus in the insistence with which the Scriptures of both testaments call for turning to God. One might almost say that conversion represents the specifically Christian understanding of the response to God's saving activity. This is a story that is renewed and repeated throughout Christian history, and in the lectures we focus on certain paradigmatic examples. However, the events that best illuminate our understanding of conversion are described in the New Testament. That is where we shall begin.

The Lectures

CHAPTER I

Converts and Proselytes

Christianity as a Jewish Religion

Let us begin at the beginning, never forgetting that the first Christian church was thoroughly, inalienably Jewish. The first seven chapters of the Book of Acts reveal what must have looked to an outside observer as a Jewish denomination, one of the immense number then subsisting. All the Jesus people are Jewish by birth and by inheritance.

Their regular meeting place is the temple, where only Jews were allowed, and it's in the temple or at least in association with the temple that the defining experience of Pentecost takes place. They are zealous in observance of Israel's religion. One of their hallmarks is their attendance at the prayers, that is, the temple liturgy. Their leader James, own brother to the one they call Messiah, we know from other sources had the nickname the Just, the Righteous—righteous, that is, in the Jewish sense of careful, heartfelt obedience to the law.

True, they were diverse in background, they were believers of Palestinian background and dispersion background, some more conservative, some more liberal, and the tension showed up sometimes as in that dispute about widows' maintenance, which led to a change in the group's administrative structure.

But for all their diversity these early believers in Jesus saw Jesus's family within the perspective of the history of Israel, within the pattern of hopes and expectations of Israel.

The New Testament frequently reflects their thoroughly Jewish sense of priorities, the concerns most on their hearts. "We had hoped that he would be the one to set Israel free," says the disillusioned disciple on the way to Emmaus. And on the Mount of Ascension the preoccupation is the same. The disciples, knowing that they stand at the threshold of a new era, ask, "Lord, will you at this time give the kingdom back to Israel?" They cannot conceive of the work of Jesus. They cannot conceive of salvation apart from the political destiny of Israel, for in Jewish terms salvation is not intelligible without the salvation of the nation. Jesus does not deny it, either. He doesn't say to them, "You have completely misunderstood what salvation is about." He simply tells them that the times and the seasons are in God's hands.

There are, of course, distinctives about this community, things that mark them out from other observant Jews. What most people, let us say, an interested Persian or Egyptian visitor to Jerusalem, would notice first was their lifestyle—communal property with special provision for vulnerable groups like widows and frequent communal meals, so that they were constantly eating in one another's houses. They had their distinctive teachings too. The sacred books of Israel spoke of the Messiah or anointed national Savior, of the Son of Man who would figure in the judgment of the world, and of the Suffering Servant, who would be a sacrifice on behalf of his people. The community identified all three figures with the recent prophet-teacher, Jesus of Nazareth. Everyone knew that he had been crucified. The community asserted that he was now alive.

But in identifying Jesus as Messiah and Son of Man and Suffering Servant, they had no idea that they had in any way changed their religion. What they had now was greater insight and depth of understanding of the religion that they had always had. They had not less delight now in the law but more. They understood better what the psalmist meant when he cried, "Oh, how I love thy law. It is my meditation all the day."

They had not less veneration for the temple but more. They remembered how Jesus had cleansed it, and reflected on the Scripture, "The zeal of your house has eaten me up." Sacrifices were for them not a thing of the past but their significance more deeply understood in the light of the servant self-offering. Jesus had ultimate significance for them, and if one word more than another summed up that significance, it was the word that they attached to his name, Messiah, Christ, the anointed of God, a name that implied the whole history of the nation of Israel and of its God-ordained outcome.

The earliest believers, that is, saw and experienced Jesus in Jewish terms, in terms of who they themselves were. That's not to say that they accepted contemporary Israel as it stood. The note of crisis, of decision, of a new age runs through all the records we have. Conversion involved no change of religion for them, but conversion was necessary nonetheless. Their reading of the sacred books would have confirmed them in the need for this and for Israel to turn again. In the Hebrew Scriptures the root *shub* occurs some 750 times in the sense of turning again or in its *hifil* form where God is the subject of restoring or bringing back.

The prophetic tradition, in particular the written prophets, Deuteronomy, and the prophetic history, constantly sound the call for Israel to turn back from its present ways or express the conviction that one day God will bring Israel back. They indicate that Israel compromises with divinities other than Yahweh and is so far from reflecting God's character, that she gives her God a bad name among other nations. Actual Israel is full of extortion and injustice and as a result of this is subject to defeat, occupation, deportation, exile.

But there's another note, and it's expressed by means of the same *shub* root. One day God will bring about a moral renewal of the nation. Indeed, there is already within it a righteous remnant, the nucleus of Israel, the earnest of its restoration and deliverance. And the personal agent of God, the Messiah, whose reign is unfailingly just and equitable, will be involved in this restoration of the nation's physical and moral well-being. And there will be an inner transformation so that people will adhere to God from their hearts, and this will herald a time of universal renewal. The Messianic Age will bless the whole world.

Let's keep these ideas in mind as we think of that earliest, very Jewish church. The framework to understand that church is there in the Synoptic Gospels. The renewal of Israel is the prime focus of Messiah's work. "You shall call his name Jesus," says the angel, "because he will save his people from their sins." That is, he will bring about the moral renewal of the nation. The Gospels show how the ministry of Jesus is heralded by that of John the Baptist. Indeed, Mark tells us that that is the beginning of the gospel, and according to those same Gospels the earliest preaching of Jesus was the same as that of John. He called for conversion, for radical change, repentance, change of mind in the light of the establishment of God's personal rule, the Kingdom of God.

The change of mind is symbolized in the rite that gave John the Dipper his nickname. John did not invent baptism. It seems to have been a purification rite for Gentiles who wished to become Jews, a naturalization ceremony for entering Israel, a symbolic washing away of the dirt of the heathen world. The revelation that John brought about was to require the baptism of Jews, to insist that the covenant people with all their knowledge of God needed his cleansing as much as any idolatrous heathen. Jews who sought baptism implicitly acknowledged their moral equivalence with the Gentile outsider.

The early chapters of Acts, which are bursting with excitement, are about the arrival of the Messianic age, the restoration and renewal of Israel. Torah, temple, even the sacrificial cultus remains, but those who recognize the Messiahship of the once-crucified Jesus, now risen, accept baptism and in so doing the need for renewal. They received the Holy Spirit, that divine activity which the prophetic writings linked with the Messianic age. They underwent a revolutionary change of lifestyle, with shared property, shared meals, and careful provision for marginalized groups, and thereby demonstrated the morally renewed nation. The community was abandoning the exploitative ways of the economically stratified society that the prophets had denounced. Here is the righteous community, the Messianic community. Here is the evidence that the restoration of Israel has begun. Everything in their present experience is explicable in terms of the accumulated traditions of Israel, its history, and its hope.

Notice that that early Jewish community did not at once go out into all the world to make disciples of all nations. We shall see that it was perhaps fortunate that it did not. There's no trace of those apostolic conferences, writers who depict the apostles as dividing the known globe between them. The few people outside Israel who are brought to Jesus—the household of Cornelius, the Samaritans, the Ethiopian eunuch—do not come through any directed effort of the church but by what the old Scot commentators would have called "special dispensations of providence, divine nudges, rather than planned operations." Furthermore, all were people already on the edge of Israel. Cornelius was a God-fearer or pious Gentile. The Samaritans were partly of Jewish descent. The Ethiopian, since he had been to Jerusalem to worship, was presumably a proselyte.

The first era of the Christian faith, with Jerusalem at its center, is so coherent in culture and tradition. The early chapters of Acts reflect a busy, growing, successful community with plenty of evidence of the Messianic restoration of Israel. Despite high priestly opposition, what else would one expect of Sadducees? There were thousands of believers coming forward, zealous, law-keeping Jews. Left to themselves the early believing community might have continued in the apostles' teaching and fellowship, breaking social bread together and attending temple prayers, praising God with favor of all the people until Jerusalem fell about their ears.

But here we come to what is arguably the single most important event in Christian history. The people concerned in it were not apostles. What happened was no part of any church strategy. We do not even know the names of the people concerned. Some Jewish believers of Cypriot or Libyan background, driven out of Jerusalem because of their connection with Stephen, came to Antioch. And unlike their colleagues elsewhere who spoke the word about Jesus to their fellow Israelites, they began to talk about Jesus to Greeks, that is, to pagans. They took a huge risk. Jesus had so far been proclaimed as Messiah, and surely the ultimate truth about Jesus was that he was the Messiah, the hope of Israel. But what could that mean to a Greek-speaking Israelite? Antiochian Gentile?

The very word Messiah when translated into Greek was odd. Why should anyone be designated the smeared one? It would take a year's course in Old Testament to find out. And supposing your Gentile friend to have the patience and the stamina to complete it, what had it all to do with him, who did not belong to the nation of which the Messiah, God's agent, was the Savior? Those believers from Cyprus and Cyrene risked a bold translation. They presented Jesus not as Messiah, though for them personally the word must have held the key to the gospel, but as Lord, the title that Antiochian pagans used for their cult divinities—and the other gods of the eastern Mediterranean. Jesus had ultimate significance, but what conveyed ultimate significance in one setting had no meaning at all in another.

This piece of cross-cultural communication, taken together with one subsequent event, changed the whole direction of the Christian faith. That event was the so-called apostolic council described in Acts 15, the watershed of that book and the charter document for Christians. At that council the apostles and elders at Jerusalem, themselves pious, law-righteous people, under the presidency of the outstandingly law-righteous brother of the Lord, agreed that followers of Jesus who were not ethnic Jews might be fully accepted within the community without the traditional signs of Jewish religious culture. They could enter Israel without becoming Jews.

Let's return to the fact that the first act of the infant church was not to go out into all the world and make disciples of every nation. It could have happened that way. After all, there was a long-standing Jewish missionary tradition. Israel had always welcomed Gentiles who recognized the God of Israel. The dispersion synagogues that we meet in Acts seemed full of such people. It was even possible for a Gentile to enter Israel, as David's ancestress Ruth the Moabitess did when she declared that her mother-in-law's God would be her own. But if males were to enter Israel, the people of the covenant, they needed to undergo circumcision, the sign of the covenant, received by ethnic Jews in the first weeks of life, received by others as a sign of their adoption. Later as we've seen, baptism was added to circumcision, adding further solemnity to the act of crossing from one world to the other.

The prophetic Scriptures indicated that in the Messianic age there would be a flood of Gentiles coming to seek the God of Israel. "Many peoples will come and say, Come, let us go up to the mountain of the Lord," the temple mountain, we notice, "to the house of the God of Jacob. The law will go forth out of Zion." Out of Zion, the temple mountain? "The word of the Lord from Jerusalem. In those days men from all languages and nations will take hold of the robe of one who is a Jew and say, Let us go with you, because we've heard that God is with you." And now, as if in fulfillment of these old prophecies, comes the news of the Gentile followers of Jesus—first in Antioch, then in the places touched by the Antiochene mission. Just what the Scriptures had indicated would happen in the Messianic age.

But we have seen that those prophecies talk of the Lord's house in Jerusalem, from which the law is to go out to all nations. It's not surprising, then, that some believers thought that the new Gentile believers should be circumcised and instructed in the law. Were they not being incorporated into Israel? And if so, should they not enter fully into their glorious heritage? The Torah was the precious jewel of Israel. Surely new believers should learn its splendor. Circumcision was the mark of the covenant. If they were to be part of the covenant people, surely they should bear it.

The way of life of a pious observant Jew was the only sort of life known to the earliest believers in Jesus. It was the way of life sanctified by the Lord himself and now practiced by the Lord's own brother and by the apostles who walked with Jesus in the years of his ministry. It's not surprising that some Christians did think like that. Nor is it surprising to find from the Epistle to the Galatians that numbers of early Gentile believers were quite ready to go along with it. Many, after all, must have been synagogue attenders for years without taking that irrevocable step of circumcision. Surely now that they knew Jesus was the time to take on the whole yoke of God, and in doing so they would be following the style of life of their teachers, the first Christians, the oldest Christians, the best Christians.

Notice Paul's reaction. It's not just disagreement, it's sheer white-hot indignation. He comes so close to incoherence that his syntax breaks down under the strain. He becomes so anatomically specific that the English versions are a little discreet about what he actually says. Paul will not even allow it as an option that someone who has been brought up as a Greek pagan should follow the lifestyle of a very good Jewish Christian. The followers of Jesus are not proselytes; they are converts. And after due deliberation the elders and apostles of Jerusalem agree.

That early rejection of the proselyte model was surely one of the crucial events in Christian history. Let's think what would have happened if the new Christians had been required to live just like the old ones. In the first place, Hellenistic social and family life would have been left entirely untouched by Christ.

Epistles like 1 Corinthians are full of tricky situations. What should one do if a pagan friend invites you to dinner and you think the meat may but perhaps may not have been offered in a temple sacrifice the day before? This was no problem for Peter, or John, or James the Just or any Jerusalem Christian, because they were not going to be invited to dinner in the first place. Observant Jews, everyone knew, did not sit down at the same table with Gentiles, with pagans. A proselyte, someone who had turned Jew, would be in the same position.

But Paul foresees Hellenistic Christians living inside Hellenistic social and family life, challenging it, disturbing it, forcing it to alter, but forcing it to alter from within, from Christian faith and Christian attitudes being expressed within it. "Yes," Paul says in effect, "go to dinner with your pagan friend. But know why and be prepared to explain on Christian grounds why you are eating or not eating that meat." Note that a whole new set of situations are building up here for Christians, situations without parallel in the experience of all previous believers, even the best of them.

In the second place, the Christian effect on Greek intellectual life would have been muted, perhaps negated altogether. Christians would have been taken out of the intellectual mainstream of Hellenistic thought, left to their own sacred books. Christ the Word made flesh in Jewish Palestine has to become flesh again in Hellenistic society, retranslated there into family and social life, into intellectual life, brought to bear on the mental and moral processes of Hellenistic civilization. Those processes were expressed in a body of teaching and literature that had taken centuries to form. Christ has now to be thought into those structures. He must be brought into conscious contact with those past centuries. The Hellenistic past had to be converted if Christ was to own the Hellenistic present.

Discipling a nation includes the turning of a nation's past toward Christ. That is why it takes generations. Anyone who enters on the work is working for the children and the grandchildren of those who are listening. In the Christian literature of the second and third and fourth centuries we see the laborious, painful but essential process of Christ entering the mental and moral processes of the Hellenistic world, of Christ being brought into contact with the literary and intellectual past of that whole civilization. It all started in Antioch when those believers from Cyprus and Cyrene took a risk and preached Jesus as Lord.

There have been many good Christians since that time who have believed that the best and the safest way for new Christians is to become as much like themselves as possible, to have the same priorities, to think the same things important, to take their Torah and circumcision. Let's make no mistake. It is the safest way. The way of a proselyte is safe. He gives up his customs and ways of thought and takes up those of another. There is a sacrifice to make. He gives up his nation, his social affiliations, his national heritage. But once he's done so, guideposts are clear. At any time of crisis there's precedent. Others have been before him. Every situation has been met before.

Converts have a much riskier life. Converts have constantly, relentlessly, to turn their ways of thought, their education, their reading, their ways of working and doing things toward Christ. These processes are shared with others to whom the convert is bound by this very heritage. This means that Christ is constantly brought into new situations, thought into new patterns of thinking.

This distinction between proselyte and convert is vital to Christian mission. Christian conversion as demonstrated in the New Testament is not about substituting something new for something old. That is in effect to move back to the proselyte model, which New Testament Christianity might have adopted but deliberately rejected. Nor is it a matter of adding something new to something old, a new set of beliefs and values to supplement those that are already in place. Conversion is about the turning of the entire social, cultural, religious inheritance toward Christ, opening them up to him. It's about turning what is already there. Christ is formed by faith among the elements that constitute the preconversion setting. That is the great adventure of Christian faith. It's always taking new shape as Christ enters new territory, as he takes flesh again in cultures where he has not walked in flesh before.

The story begun in Acts 11 in Antioch and continued through Clement of Alexandria and Origen and Augustine is the process of the conversion of the Hellenistic Roman past. In contemporary Africa, in contemporary India, in many other parts of the world we see today an analogous process as Christ is thought into those vast complexes of thought, tradition, and relationship that constitute the matrices of the new Christian world and are in their own ways as complex as anything that the Hellenistic Roman world knew. On the outcome of that process the future of our faith depends.

CHAPTER 2

A Civilization at School with Christ

The Hellenistic Experience of Christianity

When the great decision was reached to abandon the proselyte model, Gentile followers of Jesus were few in number and far from the center of Christian activity. We are used to thinking of Paul as central to New Testament Christianity. It's clear from his own life story that this was not the case. The center of New Testament Christianity is Jerusalem. It's Jerusalem that sets the norms. It's Jerusalem that sends the inspectors to Samaria and Antioch to make sure that all is in order. It's in Jerusalem that the decision about proselytes has to be taken. It's Jerusalem that had the fast-growing church, as Paul is firmly told when he comes there and tells of the conversion that he has seen in Asia Minor and Europe. "Look at the thousands of Jews who have believed!" he's told. Poor Paul couldn't claim thousands of converts. And all of them zealous for the law, fully committed people, well on their way to sanctification.

Had we a church history written in Jerusalem in those days, I doubt if it would have had more than a paragraph or so on the Gentile mission. The Gentile mission is a sideline of the early church. All of them zealous for the law. Paul himself is required to prove his Jewish credentials by undertaking to pay for a ritual sacrifice of purification. And then quite suddenly and with a minimum of preparation and warning the first model of Christianity, the model conditioned by Jerusalem, collapsed. In AD 62 James the Just, brother of the Lord, held in such high respect in Jerusalem for his conformity to the law for so long, was rejected and murdered. A few years later the Christians fled Jerusalem. The Romans destroyed the temple that has never since been rebuilt. And the Jewish state to which that early Jewish church was so intimately bound disappeared in the early holocausts of AD 70 and 135. For the future of Christianity those thousands zealous for the law, the charter Christians, ceased to matter very much. The highway for the faith lay with the descendants of those mixed-up new converts, wholly Greek in their thought, cloudy in Jewish terms about the inner meaning of Scripture, who made up the congregations of Galatia and Colossae and Corinth.

But before we leave the charter Christians let's see one more development, perhaps transitory in its original significance but a beacon light for the future, huge in its symbolism. What happened at Antioch widened the whole conception of the followers of Jesus as a community. Hitherto they had been a group of observant Messianic Jews among other observant Jews within the wider family of Israel. Insofar as they represented the righteous remnant, they were the pledge of Israel's renewal and restoration.

Of this their special lifestyle, with its common property and shared meals, was a distinctive badge. Where did the new Christians, so utterly different in their background, fit into this? Could the believers at Antioch—for it was they who were in the front line, they who must decide what was to happen in Christ's name—combine the multiethnic, multicultural church and the

Jerusalem institution of the shared meal? They did. And a new dimension thereby came into the Christian understanding of the eucharist.

The shared meal became the symbol of the multiethnic, bicultural Jesus community, and its observant Jewish members sacrificed ancestral custom at a crucial point and gave priority to the bonds of faith that formed the Jesus community over the bonds that formed the nation. It was always easier to do this in theory, as a theological exercise, or as an interpretation of Scripture resting on God's adoption of the Gentiles into Israel, than it was in practice. And many old believers, especially those who lived in Jerusalem and had no call to mix much with Gentile believers, remained unconvinced. Even Peter, who was convinced and was ready to sit down with Gentile believers at Antioch, remembered that he had another appointment when he thought that people from Jerusalem might see him doing so. "And I withstood him to his face," says Paul, "because he stood condemned."

The eucharist was the sign of the faith of Christ transcending the national community. In the process it broached that community and set up a new one. Even Peter had to decide which mattered more—the bond of faith or the bond of the nation. It should be no surprise that it was at Antioch, where the first transcending act took place, that it first became necessary for the members of the Jesus community to have a special name.

There they became Christians. The wonder of that single community forged from Jews and Gentiles, the fundamentally two made irrevocably one, shimmers through the Epistle to the Ephesians. The symbolic significance of the shared meals at Antioch remained enormous, but its immediate expression was local and temporary. Within a generation the combination of the results of the collapse of the Jewish state and the completeness of the Roman revenge that sidelined the Jerusalem church and the sheer success of the Gentile mission that brought multitudes of Gentiles to faith ensured that the Christian movement became as overwhelmingly Gentile as it had once been overwhelmingly Jewish. And the determinative cultural dynamics that shaped it and gave it identity became as essentially Hellenistic as once it had been Judaic. But the legacy of Antioch remained and it was to call to Christians of a later time. Jesus Christ was the bond of a community transcending even the most fundamental divisions of mankind.

Let us turn now to the new Hellenistic Gentile ex-pagan members of this community. They were not to become Jewish proselytes but to live actively within Hellenistic pagan society, turning its institutions and ways of thought to Christ. What changes would this bring about for them? From the point of view of a Jewish missionary, the transformation involved turning from idols to serve the living God. From the point of view of a Hellenistic Gentile attracted to the Christian faith there was a great deal in his own tradition which urged him to do just that. Certainly following Christ would involve renouncing the divinities of popular religion. But there was already an indigenous philosophical tradition, of which Socrates was the great exemplar, which undermined, even mocked traditional popular religion. Socrates had been put to death as an atheist, the very charge often leveled at Christians.

Conversion also called for high standards of moral and social behavior. It involved devotion to Jesus Christ, entry to the community of his followers. But there were many cults of particular divinities, some of them requiring significant initiation. The principle of such devotion was by no means strange. Thus far the act of conversion was intelligible within contemporary religious scenes. In fact, there was a bewildering variety of religious options available in the early centuries of the Roman Empire.

What made a difference was that those options were not held to be mutually exclusive. Above all, they did not interfere with a modicum of fairly perfunctory popular religion required for civil religion—required, that is, for everyone except Jews, the licensed exception to every rule of Roman society. The demands of the Christian community were in this respect radical and exclusive. Christians who were not ethnic Jews developed such a thoroughly Jewish attitude to traditional religious acts as to withdraw them from civil religion altogether. They were thus potentially estranged from their society at the most critical place, loyalty to the established order—a similar crux to that which Antioch had posed for Jewish believers.

Over a period of two centuries, at first sporadically and locally, later in periods of systematic endeavor, the state authorities used elements of civil religion, especially the emperor cult, as a test to identify Christians or as a control mechanism when they got too numerous or noticeable. This in turn increased the Christian sense of community and the identification of becoming a follower of Christ with joining a community. That community, the church, was increasingly seen as a single entity, even as the empire was a single entity. Whereas Paul talks principally of the churches when he's referring to actual communities, the literature of the second and third centuries speaks rather of the church. This didn't mean that Christians rejected societal ties. That they were loyal, law-keeping, tax-paying citizens concerned for the emperor's safety and the security of the imperial frontiers and praying for both was a claim they constantly offered. And all this was implicitly recognized when, in the days of Constantine, the empire found it desirable to accommodate to the church.

Paul, who more than anyone else had enunciated the idea of a single community made out of hitherto irreconcilable entities, retained the idea of turning that had been displayed in the Hebrew prophetic Scriptures about conversion. The holy people of God are being transformed from a life of evil into what in principle they already are. The peril is that they may be conformed to the norms of the surrounding society. A parallel runs through the Johannine writings, where the world is used as the index of everything that opposes God. An overwhelmingly Hellenistic Roman church was bound to lose some of the resonances of the Israelite Scriptures, however sincerely claimed and devotedly read.

They had another religious model for conversion at hand within Hellenistic culture. Indeed, it seems that the very word "conversion" has passed into its present use by way of translating the Greek technical term *metabole*, used by the philosophical schools for the decision to embrace the life of philosophy. In this there is a vast gulf between the life of the true philosopher and the life of the generality of humankind.

Those who embrace the philosopher's life do so as a result of enlightenment. Enlightenment is instantaneous, even if preceded by a long preparation. There is no middle point between wisdom and folly. Philosophic enlightenment and subsequent pursuit of the higher life formed one model for Christian conversion in the Hellenistic world, just as the restored, renewed Israel did for the earliest Jerusalem church.

The literature of the second and third centuries contains some autobiographical statements about conversion and many insights into how those seeking conversion or teaching others about the Christian community went about their work. For instance, there's a work by Justin Martyr in the middle of the second century that gives a circumstantial account of his own conversion. That conversion springs directly from his pursuit of philosophy as a means of achieving *metabole*. As the story begins, Justin describes the vision of God, which for Plato is the end of philosophy. Philosophy, that is to say, is not an academic attainment but a religious quest. Justin attends a variety of schools with increasing disillusionment. He abandons those teachers who wanted to settle their fees in advance as being no philosophers at all.

Justin comes to find that there is an inability of all the philosophical schools to discover ultimate reality. Then, in a dialogue formulated with an "old man," he is pointed to the Hebrew prophets, and is urged to pray for enlightenment, since only through God and his Christ can these things be understood. And then the old man disappears. "But straightway," says Justin,

a flame was kindled in my soul, and a love of the prophets and of those men who are friends of Christ possessed me. And while revolving his words in my mind, I found this philosophy to be safe and profitable. Thus and for this reason I am a philosopher. Moreover, I wish that all making a resolution similar to my own do not keep themselves away from the words of the Savior. They possess a terrible power in themselves and are sufficient to inspire those who turn aside from the path of rectitude with awe, while the sweetest rest is afforded to those who make diligent practice of them. If then, you have any concern for yourself and are eagerly looking for salvation and if you believe in God, you may become acquainted with the Christ of God and after being initiated live a happy life.

Several features of Justin's account are worth notice. First, observe that his quest begins entirely within his own pre-Christian tradition. There's nothing exotic about it. The goals are the time-honored Greek goals: purification by wisdom and the vision of God as the end of the philosophic life. This is not, of course, to say that those goals were widely adopted in the community. On the contrary, Justin becomes increasingly frustrated by finding that even professional philosophers are rarely consumed with the quest. And even after meeting the old man who represents the Christian message, Justin's pilgrimage continues for some way along the traditional path. This is true of the method by which he gradually becomes convinced of the Christian worldview—that is, the Socratic dialog. It's equally true of the topics that are discussed with the old man, the nature of the soul, even though the outcome of the argument is demonstration of the bankruptcy of the traditional sources on such vital topics.

But in the process Justin is introduced to a new factor, a source of knowledge outside the traditional sources, the Christian Scriptures. More particularly the prophets of Israel were seen as depicting in advance the life, ministry, death, and resurrection of Jesus Christ. The stress on the Hebrew prophets rather than on the explicitly Christian documents may seem remarkable until one remembers that the Hebrew Scriptures formed the only body of literature at that time that could claim a comparable antiquity with the greatest works of priests.

Christian apologists frequently sought to show that Moses lived before Plato or that some of Plato's best ideas could have been derived from Isaiah. This clinging to antiquity was important, because in a society that distinguished itself from the barbarians by its possession of a corpus of learning and literature, convinced that every important idea had been canvassed and explored within that corpus, there was little room for ideas of recent origin. It's the antiquity of Christianity that is important, and the antiquity depends on the Hebrew Scriptures.

So Justin and his contemporaries read the prophets and the other Israelite writings in Greek, and by using them as a philosophical sourcebook adopted them into the Greek universe of ideas. The process brought into that universe ideas and influences hitherto unknown, ideas sometimes incompatible with it. But the new ideas are brought into the preexisting framework and are formulated by the preexisting methods. And the authoritative nature of the new sources coexists with the axiomatic nature of the existing framework. In other words, we receive endless tension but also a deep desire for reconciliation.

Justin's conversion, in fact, leads him to attempt the conversion of the whole world of thought in which he has been brought up. It leads him to take the Scriptures into intellectual areas outside the original concern of the scriptural writers. Thus, he recognizes in the title logos used in the fourth Gospel not simply the designation of the divine Son as the Word but the identification of the divine Son with its other sense—reason. This enables him not only to bring the God of the Scriptures and the Father of the Lord Jesus Christ into the history of Hellenistic culture. It enables him to use the Scriptures as a criterion of truth within the philosophical tradition itself. Socrates and all others who spoke according to logos, that is to reason, and suffered for it did so by means of the Logos, the capital L Logos, the divine Word, the Son of God. They were, Justin is bold to say, Christians before Christ, because they participated in the Logos of God.

The subsequent history of Christianity in the Roman Empire is the story of that continuing interaction of the Hellenistic Roman inheritance of language, philosophy, and law with ideas and expressions that belonged to the Hebraic tradition and are given fixity by their embodiment in the Scriptures. And all are underlaid by the conviction of the ultimate significance of Christ. The old inheritance is reshaped, but it's not abandoned. The new ideas and expressions are put to new uses. The figure of Jesus Christ retains ultimate significance as in the earliest phase of Christianity, but it's now ultimate significance not within the expectations deriving from the long and peculiar history but within those of the Greek intellectual tradition and amid the religious quests of the Hellenistic Roman world.

At the end of his pilgrimage Justin remains a philosopher. We have an account of his martyrdom, showing that at that time he was still presenting Christianity as a teacher of philosophy. He had found in Christ and the Hebrew Christian Scriptures what he was looking for when he set out to seek *metabole* among the philosophical schools. He found by his own account, quoted earlier, the path of right living, rest of mind, acquaintance with God, a happy life. All these things belong to the contemporary philosopher's quest.

Justin's story leads us to a number of reflections on this second chapter of Christian history, the encounter of the Christian faith with the Hellenistic Roman world. Notice how the story begins within that world's religious quests, how he finds Christian answers to his pre-Christian questions, how he uses Christian source materials, the Hebrew Scriptures in translation, the Gospels, and brings them into a realm of discourse, the common themes of Greek philosophy, which is quite different from those of their origin, but where they have become very quickly at home.

Justin's conversion, that is, is not a purely personal affair. It's part of the conversion of the culture. And it's not affected by replacement, by substituting a new culture for the old. Nor is it a piecemeal process of replacing certain pre-Christian institutions with Christian ones. The old framework is too comprehensive, too all-embracing for that. It is a whole system and must be brought into obedience to Christ as a whole. And that requires a more radical process performed from inside the culture, applying the Christian sources, the living tradition about Christ and the Scriptures associated with him, to a series of intellectual and social situations that arise from the pre-Christian agenda. That agenda itself arose from the accumulation of the Hellenistic past from centuries of literature, of religion, of philosophical endeavor, of the development of shared ways of thinking and reasoning and choosing.

Let us never forget that we are constituted by our past. To lose our past is to enter a state of amnesia; to lose our memory is to lose our identity, our certainty, our ability to form assured relationships. It is useless to attempt to repress the past. The past cannot be substituted. It has to be converted. Translating into modern African terms one might say, "We dare not abandon the ancestors. If we do, they will come back and haunt us. Christ must take care of our past if he is to rule our present unchallenged."

The story of the second, the third, the fourth, the fifth century of Mediterranean Christianity is the story of the conversion of the Hellenistic past. In that story Justin is but one participant, whose story we know rather better than some others. A generation after his death a boy was born in a Christian home in Alexandria who was to accelerate the process and bring a new grandeur to it with the sheer comprehensiveness of his attempt to think Christ into the whole encyclopedia of Greek knowledge, to apply the Scriptures to the whole range of intellectual inquiry. I believe that we should honor that boy, Origen by name, as the father of mission studies, the first person to catch the whole vision of its panoramic scope.

And let's remember that it was scholarship under the cross. When he was sixteen, his father was taken to martyrdom. Many times, Origen himself nearly suffered the same fate. Many of those he trained in the Scriptures did so, sometimes before they had sealed their faith in baptism. In his late sixties he was beaten, tortured, and imprisoned and not long afterward died.

But Origen knew that the intellectual and academic world of the museum and the lecture hall and the worlds of philosophic and literary discourse, which were at their height in Alexandria, fell within the redemption of Christ and must be won for him. He tells us,

> Think of the tabernacle made in the wilderness. Where did all the gold for it come from? How were the cherubim, speaking signs of the invisible presence of the Lord, constructed? From gold taken from the Egyptians. The curtains of the tabernacle were made from Egyptian cloth. Christian effort should be directed to taking the things used in the heathen world and fashioning from them materials fit for the worship and glorification of God.

Once more we learn that conversion is not substituting something new for something old but turning toward Christ the materials that are already there. Origen, the first Christian systematic theologian, the first systematic textual critic, the developer though not the inventor of the biblical commentary, marks a new stage in the conversion of Hellenistic culture.

Paul was its first great figure, with his breathtaking innovations, like seizing the idea of the pleroma of eons that separated the transcendent God of Hellenistic assumption from the phenomenal world and identifying that pleroma with Christ.

But in the end Paul was a missionary and a foreign missionary, and he thinks and he talks like one. Successful as he has been with the degree of cultural adaptation that he made, he is aware that he was circumcised on the eighth day of the tribe of Benjamin and belongs to the cultivated olive, into which Hellenistic Christianity is only a graft.

Justin is on the inside of Hellenistic Christianity, a convert, who has found in the Christian Scriptures a source that makes sense in Hellenistic terms, with which to critique his intellectual inheritance and offer criteria by which to test it, both to affirm and to denounce. Origen, born in a Christian home, brought up on the Scriptures and also with the best available education in the whole range of indigenous sources, has the confidence to undertake the rethinking of that whole cultural inheritance in Christian terms.

We've no time to consider the shape of the Hellenistic Roman Christianity that emerged. Let's note only that it was as culturally coherent, that it made sense in terms of contemporary discourse, just as fully as the original Jewish Christianity had done within its own. It developed some features that have remained features of later Christianity. It translated Christian convictions into the categories of Greek philosophical discourse. It sharpened and defined them according to the practices of Greek philosophical debate. It reached consensus by processes of consultation derived from Greek civic administration and government. And it codified the results according to the principles of Roman law. The result was orthodoxy: canons of correct, considered, consensual Christian belief adopted after debate and consideration.

We cannot imagine the apostles and elders of Jerusalem doing this. Jewish concerns have always been about what a person is and does rather than what that person believes, about orthopraxy rather than orthodoxy. But orthodoxy was a direct result of the Christian entrance into the Hellenistic world, for not only did Christianity have an impact on the Hellenistic world. That world had a substantial impact on Christianity. It raised issues for Christians, started questions for them that they had never had to face before. We can see the process beginning within the New Testament itself. We can see the words of Jesus in the Synoptic Gospels to the first Jewish apostles where we find the key words are "the kingdom of God" and "the Son of Man." Read Paul's letters to the Gentile churches and we have a mere handful of incidental references to the kingdom of God and no mention whatever of the Son of Man.

The Hellenistic world needed a new conceptual vocabulary, a translation of the gospel—nay, its transposition into a different key. And in the process of translation, in the transposition of the message into Greek categories, questions about Christ that were forced by those very categories, that in terms of traditional Jewish piety might seem to be secondary or even irreverent in the asking, become matters of major significance, questions about the eternity of the Son, for instance.

Using the Greek language and Greek habits of thought forced people to consider how to think of Christ according to the category of *ousia*. No single text could be found in Scripture to address this. How the fathers of Nicaea would have loved to find a single word of Scripture that would have settled the issue before them! It was necessary to follow the canons of Greek thought through to a Christian conclusion. Do you mean one thing, or do you mean another in application to the whole body of Scripture, to the sense of Scripture, to determine whether in fact Christ was the eternal Son of one substance with the Father or whether he was a demigod like Heracles. In other words, the act of translation into another language and into the intellectual forms of another culture and the painful wrestling with the consequences that followed led to new discoveries about who Christ is.

When those people from Cyprus and Cyrene wanted to share their joy in Jesus with their pagan friends in Antioch and move from proclaiming Jesus as Messiah with all its rich Hebrew resonance to the title Kyrios Jesus, it must have seemed to many at the very least an impoverishment of the gospel, at worst a perilous and misleading identification. In the providence of God it was to lead not only to a great intellectual adventure but to a permanently enriching discovery of who and what the Messiah was.

CHAPTER 3

Barbarian Christianity

The Birth of Western Christendom

The story of Christian history that we have begun to follow depends not simply on geographical expansion but on cross-cultural expansion, and the perspective that we've adopted sees Christian history as a serial process of interaction with successive cultures. We have now considered two such processes. We saw that the initial spread of the Jesus movement in the Palestinian Jewish community where Jesus himself lived and worked produced a body of faith and life entirely coherent in terms of Jewish history and Jewish religion. We saw that a cross-cultural diffusion that involved a massive act of translation and transposition, initially it seems through the enterprise of some Jerusalem refugees in Antioch, led to the word about Jesus the Messiah of Israel being heard in the Hellenistic world as the Word of the Lord Jesus Christ. The outcome was wholly intelligible in Hellenistic terms, because the community abandoned the Jewish proselyte model and sought one that attempted to transform society from the inside and took the word about Christ into the realms of Hellenistic social and intellectual life.

We might have noted also that the movement across the ethnic Hellenistic cultural frontier took place only just in time, for within a very short period the first Judaic model of Christianity for all practical purposes disappeared. Cross-cultural diffusion has been the life blood of historic Christianity, for Christianity, unlike Islam, has a curious tendency to wither in its heartlands and find new growth beyond them, to decay at the center and expand at the periphery.

We noted also that the experience of entry into a new culture and a new world of thought expanded the understanding of Christ. That process posed new questions that required an answer. When the Word was made flesh, it was under the conditions of Jewish Palestine, and the first believers who shared those conditions declared his glory in terms of the history and hope of Israel. When Christ was received by faith in congregations of the eastern Mediterranean, he began to take flesh again in a setting shaped by Greek philosophy, Roman law, and Levantine devotion.

This also meant that Greek questions would be asked about him. It was not enough to say that he was seated at the right hand of God. It was necessary to explore what that meant about his relationship with God and if that relationship were to be expressed in Greek categories such as ousia and hypostasis. It meant using the categories and methods of indigenous intellectual discourse to explore what Christians really believed. It meant reaching consensus on the outcome, formulating that outcome rather as Roman law courts would formulate it.

By such processes Christian faith made its home in the Roman Empire and in the Greek tradition that that empire had adopted. With that tradition had come a twofold division of humankind that was as comprehensive in its effects as the old Jewish distinction between the nation of Israel and the nations, the Gentiles. This was the distinction that we find Paul himself alluding to between Greeks and barbarians. Greek was not here an ethnic term. It had nothing to do with where you were born, with your race, or your skin color. It was a cultural term. It stood for those who spoke Greek, who thought and read and built and lived in a certain way, who shared a certain universe of ideas common to all civilized peoples.

Those who did not were barbarians, *barbaroi*, people whose language was all baba. That is what the word means. And to the imagination of Roman folk what lay beyond the frontiers of the empire from the Atlantic to the Danube were the barbarians, fierce, unmanageable, and as the sand by the seashore for multitude—peoples who, if the imperial frontiers were to collapse, would destroy all civilization. Christians of the Roman Empire shared the attitudes of their non-Christian colleagues toward the barbarians.

Tertullian tells us that in his day when state persecution of Christians was still active, Christians prayed for the delay of the end, and therefore they prayed for the upholding of the imperial frontiers. Tertullian clearly believed that when those frontiers broke and the barbarians came in, the tribulation would begin. And it was right that Christians pray to be spared that.

The actual outcome was rather different. The imperial frontiers did collapse, and the tribal peoples to the north did overrun much of the western Roman Empire. And the effect was indeed devastating and did indeed weaken and in some areas obliterate Christianity. The Christian peoples of North Africa, for instance, faded under the impact.

But another process was at work too. Slowly, painfully in a development that took many centuries to accomplish, another of those cross-cultural diffusions took place, which changed the ethnic and cultural shape of Christianity. More and more of the tribal peoples of the north and west came under Christian influence and slowly and painfully entered the Christian faith. We suggested above that the Gentile mission was never the main enthusiasm of the Jerusalem church but rather a sideline. Similarly, commending Christ among the barbarians was never a central concern of the Christian empire. But the time came when the fact that some Christians had engaged in such work both transformed Christianity and secured the future for the faith. For Christianity once more went into decline in the areas of its apparent strength. Areas like the eastern Mediterranean and North Africa, Egypt and Syria, the rich provinces of the east that had seen the heights of Christian endurance, the greatest glories of Christian sanctity and scholarship, came under Muslim rule. The western Roman Empire passed into tribulation and devastation. Once more the faith had been saved by its cross-cultural diffusion.

The culture gap between the old Christians and the new required another transposition, another change of key for Christian life. Christianity had developed as the face of a largely urban-based society with developed literacy and technology and communications and a common lifestyle. The new Christians were peasant subsistence farmers or military adventurers living by fighting or semi-settled raiders. Let's take one or two examples that the Christian literature of those centuries gives us of the factors that led people among the barbarians to adopt the faith of Christ. We'll see that we're a long way from Justin, searching the philosophical schools for a teacher who would lead him to the vision of God.

In terms of political significance few conversions can have been of more importance than that of Clovis, king of the Franks in Gaul, of which an account is provided by Gregory of Tours. Here we see a barbarian pagan ruler supported by a military caste of the same mold, controlling territory that had long been settled by a Christian population who had shared in Roman civilization. The king's wife is a Christian, and he has married into the subject people. And the Christian queen secures the baptism of their newborn son. The child dies almost immediately afterward. This confirms Clovis in his view of the powerlessness of the religion practiced by his wife and by his subjects. Clovis is eventually brought to affirm the Christian religion when he is delivered from a desperate military situation, when prayer to the Christian God was his last available resource, when he had tried everything else and failed. Even so, he is reluctant to accept baptism as the officer corps of the army were likely to oppose it.

To his surprise he finds that the officer corps has been swayed by the same factors as himself, and so he is induced to make the change. His baptism is followed, Gregory says, by that of three thousand of his military followers. Gregory, who himself belongs to the indigenous Gallo-Roman Christian gentry, recognized that this momentous conversion of Clovis took place in terms of the traditional expectations and the traditional goals of Clovis's old religion.

There's a better-known story given by Bede about the conversion of the king of the Kingdom of Northumbria in northern England. The kingdom was the result of the invasions and concentrated settlement of Teutonic peoples in large areas of northern Brittain. Edwin the king has, like Clovis, a Christian wife, a princess from a Christian kingdom to the south. He hears the preaching of her chaplain and is personally well disposed toward Christianity. But he cannot make any move until he is sure of the support of his leading men. He therefore calls a council at which the question of what Bede calls "the new doctrine and the new worship" is proposed. One of those who speaks first is a priest of the old religion, and he gives his vote for Christianity, and this is why. "None of your people," he's talking to the king, "has applied himself more diligently to the worship of our gods than I have. And yet there are many who receive greater favor from you and are more preferred than I and are more prosperous in all their undertakings. Now if the gods were good for anything, they would rather forward me, who has been careful to serve them. It remains therefore if, on examination, you find the new doctrines which are now preached to us better and more efficacious, we immediately receive them without delay."

Here's one good reason for religious change—the failure of the existing religious resources to meet acknowledged goals. One may add in passing that perhaps very few people are ever converted from one religion to another. Rather, the conversion is from agnosticism when you've reached the end of the resources of the old.

Another speaker at the council is a senior warrior. "The present life of man, O king, seems to me in comparison of that time which is unknown to us. Like the swift flight of a sparrow through a room where you sit at supper in winter with your commanders and ministers and a good fire in the midst while storms of rain and snow prevail abroad. The sparrow, flying in at one door and immediately out of the other, while he's inside is safe from the wintry storm. But after a short space of fair weather vanishes out of your sight into the dark winter from which he'd emerged. So this life of man appears for a short space, but of what went before or what was to follow we are utterly ignorant. If, therefore, this new doctrine contains something more certain, it seems justly to deserve to be followed."

The speaker, you will have noticed, has identified an item in the Christian teaching that is new to him and at least specific where traditional belief was vague. It was not necessarily the most important part of the Christian proclamation from the point of view of the preacher, but it was the part that registered most forcibly with the auditor as meeting its own need. And so the council votes for the new religion, and the priest who had spoken first led the profanation of the altars that he'd formerly served. "And the king with all the nobility of the nation and a large number of the common sort," says Bede, "received the faith and the washing of regeneration." They were baptized.

Now I don't suppose a shorthand writer was present for those speeches, but nevertheless they ring true in terms of the conversion process as a whole. In northern Europe conversion is not something for individual decision, even the individual decision of a strong king. It's for corporate discussion and consensual action. It relates, after all, to communal matters, to ancestral custom, to the generally accepted modes of life within a community. There's no question here of conversion leading to entrance to a new community. Conversion simply reconstitutes the perceptions of the existing community.

What we are witnessing here is the birth of territorial Christianity, the origin of the idea of the Christian nation, the nation of which every member is a member of the church. Not Constantine, nor Theodosius could have envisaged the territorial Christianity that developed in the north. The Roman Empire had too much diversity, too many interest groups, too much inbuilt pluralism. The last community within the Roman Empire to accept the Christian faith was the senate, the old aristocracy. It is among the northern peoples with no division of religious custom from profane custom that territorial Christianity necessarily emerges. A single people must have a single custom. If custom is no longer working satisfactorily, it may be revised, but it will still bind the whole troop. Christianity begins its entry into the thought world and the life experience of the northern cultivators as once it had that of Hellenistic Roman society. It's an act made in terms of traditional perceptions and produces a change in the central symbols of the society. The new tradition associated with those symbols then begins a long continuing process of interaction with that society.

We are witnessing here the birth of Western Christianity, and I verily believe that some features of Western Christianity today cannot be understood without an understanding of this process. I therefore make no apology for devoting one of our chapters to it. It's proper to mention, incidentally, that the Western lands are only part of the story of barbarian Christianity, that there was another equally dramatic and highly influential story unfolding among the peoples eastward, which was to issue in Slavonic Christianity.

We have time, however, to look only at what happened to the Western barbarians from whom people like myself are descended. And you'll note that one important aspect of their approach to Christianity is its impact on customary law. Christianity is something that is going to affect communal life. It's going to have an impact on customs, on festivals, on sacrifices. The decision, therefore, whether to adopt it or not must be whether doing so will be for the benefit of the group or the community as a whole.

The situation may be illustrated from another story, the conversion of Iceland, which did not take place until about AD 1000. Iceland is particularly interesting because it had no monarchy, no central authority. It was a sort of democracy with an assembly of heads of families.

The arrival of the first missionary, a Saxon, to Iceland brought a number of conversions in one part of the island, but it also brought intense resistance. In a short time the island was split between Christian families and families adhering to the old religion, and there was a prospect of war between them. A way out of the impasse was found when one of the leading Christians proposed arbitration. Let one of the most generally respected elders choose which way the community should follow. They chose an elder, and of course, being an old man he was a pagan. For two days and two nights he sat in darkness, a cloak over his head, while the whole assembly waited. Then he arose, cast off the cloak, and announced that the community would be Christian— that they would keep Christmas and Easter as festivals, that they would immediately abandon the practice of exposing female children, and would, after a six-month transitional period for those who wished it, abandon shrine worship.

The supporters of the old religion felt betrayed and complained, but they accepted the verdict. What no one suggested was that some people should follow the Christian custom and some should follow the old law. Such a position was a recipe for civil war. A single people must follow a single code of custom.

I do not think we have sufficiently grappled with this aspect of the conversion period in northern Europe nor the extent to which it has permanently marked Western Christianity. One important aspect of Christianity in northern Europe was that it provided a sure base for customary law. Tribal societies are bound by custom, and that custom is held in place by spiritual sanctions. The Hellenistic Roman world like the modern world could find ways of distinguishing between the sacred and the secular realms. Tribal societies cannot. They can make no such separation. The spiritual world and the natural world continually interpenetrate.

So to change the custom of a primal society is to go to its very heart. Custom is its heart. Custom is its life blood. So to adopt new festivals goes to the heart of a society. Adopting a prohibition of a long-standing practice, like exposure of female children, is a critical decision involving spiritual powers.

Introducing a new taboo, such as prohibiting fighting on Sunday among these military peoples, is recognizing a new and powerful spiritual force. Spiritual force was, in fact, often one of the determining factors in whether and when a society became Christian. Time and again the decision for Christianity was delivered because it seemed to offer superior power and protection to that offered by the traditional sources. These were people who lived harsh, dangerous, and usually brief lives, full of daily peril. What they most needed was the assurance of protection. Power and protection were at the heart of traditional religion. The traditional religion was not very effective at supplying them.

Note how both Clovis, the powerful military adventurer, and Coifi, the traditional priest, eventually decide that the God of Christians is to be followed because He is more powerful, that He is the superior deliverer. The pantheon of the Teutonic peoples represented the very gods at war among themselves. The very gods are temporary. In the day of Ragnarok or Goetterdammerung, the twilight of the gods, they will wipe one another out, and they will be succeeded by other divinities, as Ukteracile, the tree of the world, brings forth new fruit. The Christian God, one God, all powerful, ruler of history, ruler of wind and rain, ruler of harvests, ruler of all—if you could but trust him—offered better security, especially if prudence also urged that farming was likely to be a better way of life than fighting.

And so we watch the gradual transition in the grave goods of Scandinavia and Scotland, how gradually the graves with little metal emblems of the hammer of Thor give place to little metal emblems of the cross of Christ. There are times of transition too where people play safe, and you find in the grave both the cross and the hammer, and occasionally an emblem that might be either a cross or a hammer. And we remember that in

Iceland there was a Viking called Helge the Half Christian, who worshiped Christ on land because he recognized the power of Christ there, but Thor, once he got into his boat, for Thor was in charge of the winds.

But in general the peoples of the West saw the God of the Christians as the most likely source of the power needed to withstand their enemies, natural and spiritual, that surrounded them on every side. That power was found in the God of the Christians by Clovis on the field of battle. It was found by many a peasant farmer in his prayers for a good harvest. The local spirit shrines had been the trustees of spiritual power. That trusteeship now passed to the church, a bigger entity, as befitted a bigger God than the peoples of the north had ever known.

What was it like to be a praying Christian, to be even a missionary in a setting such as this, to be entering in Christ's name against the principalities and powers of a spirit-packed universe? We have plenty of missionary writings that tell us. To close, I've chosen one that seems to me to give an authentic flavor of barbarian Christianity. It's a hymn or a chant from Ireland, where it has long been associated with Patrick, the apostle of Ireland, and is often called St. Patrick's Breastplate. A version of it appears in many modern hymnbooks, but it's a very milk-and-water version, and I thought you might like to hear it in the original or as near the original as I can get it in English. I wish I had time to speak of Patrick himself.

He is in many ways a striking example of a devout Christian of this period and place, very brave and humble, a direct sort of Celtic Christian, who hears the voice of God in dreams and visions and has appalling experiences and startling deliverances. The Devil himself descends on his chest and then miraculously departs as Patrick calls out the powerful word that God himself has given him for the purpose.

Actually the hymn I'm going to quote is probably not by Patrick at all, but by another missionary a century or so later. But let me, all the same, quote the little tag of explanation that some Irish scribe has put on it, because it does tell us something of the world in which these Christians lived. Here is the scribe.

Patrick made this hymn. It was made in the time of Leery, Son of Neil. The cause of its composition, however, was to protect him and his monks against deadly enemies that lay in wait for the clerics. This is a breastplate of faith for the protection of body and soul against devils and men and vices. When anyone shall repeat it every day with diligent intentness on God, devils will not dare face him. It shall be a protection to him against every poison and envy. It shall be a defense to him against sudden death. It will be a breastplate to his soul after death. Patrick sang this hymn when ambuscades were laid against his coming by Leery that he might not go to Tara to show the faith. This is the missionaries on a missionary journey. Here are the powers of darkness seeking to stop him proclaiming the word.

There's an ambush, and then it appeared before those lying in ambush that Patrick and his monks were wild deer with a fawn following them. So Patrick and his monks and the fawn that follows (think who the fawn might be) pass on their way, and only after they've gone do the ambushers realize that they have lost their prey. Its name is "The Deer's Cry."

And now to the hymn. Imagine this missionary getting up in the morning, thinking of the various perils that he's going to face during the day. Binding on his spiritual armor piece by piece, invoking the Trinity, using the words hammered out in Hellenistic times in the creeds, not now as an attempt to define the truth but because words of truth about God are words of power.

See how he passes to the person and work of Christ and appropriates it for himself and then how he looks upon the heavenly powers—archangels and cherubim, far superior in the end to the devil and his angels, should they appear, as happened now and again to Patrick. See how he passes to the great church, of which he is a member and representative, and remembers that the apostles and prophets, the saints and the martyrs, all the holiest people of the present day, are all his allies, are all on his side.

He thinks of the powers of nature, of heaven and earth, that will condition the work he has to do today, and remembers that they too are creatures of his God. He can claim them on his side. Then he thinks of God's protection in its detail. And he faces up to all the worst things that can happen to him today— temptation, weakness, malice, witchcraft, demonic influence, cruelty, heathenism, heresy, idolatry, magic, accidents by fire or water, poison or mishap. And then he turns to Christ who will be his companion today in all these perils, like the fawn that followed Patrick.

> I arise today through a mighty strength, the invocation of the Trinity through belief in the threeness, through confession of the oneness towards the Creator. Get up from your mat towards the Creator.
>   I arise today through the strength of Christ with his baptism, through the strength of his crucifixion with his burial, through the strength of his resurrection with his ascension, through the strength of his descent for the judgment of doom.

I arise today through the strength of the love of the cherubim, in obedience of angels, in the service of the archangels, in the hope of resurrection to meet with reward, in the prayers of patriarchs (*I think that's the translation, though a possible variant would be "in the prayers of my ancestors"*), in the predictions of the prophets, in preachings of apostles, in face of confessors, in innocence of holy virgins, in the deeds of righteous people.

I arise today through the strength of heaven, light of sun, brilliance of moon, splendor of fire, speed of lightning, swiftness of wind, depth of sea, stability of earth, firmness of rock.

I arise today through God's strength to pilot me, God's might to uphold me, God's wisdom to guide me, God's eye to look before me, God's ear to hear me, God's word to speak for me, God's hand to guard me, God's way to lie before me, God's shield to protect me, God's host to secure me *(and now he thinks of the perils)*, against snares of devils, temptations of vices, inclinations of nature, against everyone who shall wish me ill *(because of somebody's wishing you ill, cursing you in their heart, that has objective power, and you need protection against that just as you do against these internal perils of temptation and vice and unbelief)*.

I summon today all these powers between me and these evils *(now he thinks of all the things that can happen to him)*, against every cruel, merciless power that may oppose my body or my soul *(here's Patrick trying to get to Tara and Leery determined to stop him)*, against incantations of false prophets *(because they'll be out and you'll have the old priests out with incantations)*, against black laws of heathenry, against false laws of heretics, against craft of idolatry, against the spells of women and smiths and wizards. *(In Ireland certain women were known to have particular power; it occurs in Iceland too; the last great opponent of the faith is a prophetess. Smiths refers to the blacksmiths, the specialist workmen. If you know your Wagner, you know how important the smith is in this background. The wizards are opposed to every knowledge that endangers the body or the soul.)*

Christ to protect me today against poison, against burning, against drowning, against wounding, so that there may become abundance of reward.

> Christ with me, Christ before me,
> Christ behind me, Christ in me,
> Christ beneath me, Christ above me,
> Christ on my right, Christ on my left,
> Christ where I lie down, Christ where I sit,
> Christ where I arise,
> Christ in the heart of every man who thinks of me,
> Christ in the mouth of every man who speaks of me.

Then you know fort and word can't do you any harm. If they're speaking or thinking of Christ, what harm can they do to Christ's servant?

 Christ in every eye that sees me, Christ in every ear that hears me.

 I arise today through a mighty strength, the invocation of the Trinity, through belief in the threeness, through confession of the oneness towards the Creator. Salvation is of the Lord. Salvation is of the Lord. Salvation is of Christ. May thy salvation, O Lord, be ever with us.

CHAPTER 4

Christianity without Christendom
The Making of Modern Christianity

Though Western church history is the area of Christian history that's received the most attention, it's possibly also the most misunderstood. There are two or three aspects of it which may need special attention because of their impact on later Christianity and especially that of the southern continents, which must surely dominate modern church history from this time on.

The first may be quickly disposed of. As we have seen, the West adopted Christianity into its frameworks of customary and tribal law. There are many relics of this today. For instance, it's why we still have state churches today in northern Europe when very few people go to them. There's no secular enthusiasm in northern Europe for disestablishing the state churches. They are still necessary to tribal custom and have important ritual and constitutional functions. We even retain a former sacred monarchy, descended from the Christian portrait of a monarch as the Lord's anointed ruling as the humble vassal of the King of Kings, which replaced the old tribal idea of the monarch as a descendant of Wotan, god of war.

But the interaction with tribal law reinforced by the adoption by the tribes under Christian influence of Roman law had a reflex action that helped to reshape Christianity itself. We saw how the transposition of Christianity into a Hellenistic setting and the translation of its central affirmations into Greek raised for the first time new questions about Christ that needed Greek answers. In the same way the transposition of the face into a northern Europe bound by tribal and Roman law posed new questions about those Christian affirmations. Let me just offer one illustration of how Christian thought began to interact with the existing institutions.

It leads, for instance, to a more explicit working out of the doctrine of the atonement than early Christian writers thought necessary. The interest in the doctrine of the atonement I think lies very much in the background of Western customary law. The key figure is the twelfth-century archbishop of Canterbury, Anselm. His classic book is *Cur Deus Homo*, literally Why God Man. The disobedience of Adam and Eve, according to Anselm, created a state of estrangement from God that was conveyed to their descendants. The state of events could not be removed until compensation was provided. But humanity, the debtor, did not have the means to pay. Only God had the means. But humanity had the debt. So God became human in order to pay the compensation.

Notice the underlying assumptions. Offenses require compensation equal in weight. Relationships depend on this retributive principle. Second, both in commission of offenses and compensation for offenses the kin of the offender are liable. If the kin, for instance, offer compensation equal to the offense, the offended has to accept the compensation.

Two different sources have been proposed for Anselm's assumptions. One is Roman law applied from all time in Latin

Christianity to church discipline as the basis of penance. The other idea I think more likely is that it comes from Germanic law, the law in which relations were soldered by compensation or by retribution on the kin of the offender. Whichever is true, or if indeed both contribute to the idea, the ideas of Anselm obviously rang true in this world of Latin Christendom.

The difficulties with this doctrine of the atonement appear only in later days when the grip of legal systems on theology are less and when the idea of kinship is itself threatened by new ideas about individual relationships. Related to this is the fact that the legal framework that Latin Christianity applied to theology made possible a new exercise that hadn't occurred to early Christian writers and has apparently not often occurred to Greek Christians—the exercise of systematic theology, codifying all orthodox belief in the way that laws can be codified, developing those doctrines along lines that legal theory worked on. Two of the grandest theological monuments of the West are exactly outworkings of this principle—Aquinas's *Summa Theologica* and Calvin's *Institutes of the Christian Religion.*

The second aspect to which I draw attention here is the new dimension that Western Christianity gives to conversion. At one time conversion was associated with entering a new community of the faithful, but the special processes by which Western Europe became Christian meant that there was no new community to join. The community *is* the church. The community is the community of all the faithful. But everyone realizes that that community is at the very best a poor reflection of the community of Christ. At any given time it is at best a compromise, at worst a mockery. Society manifestly does not reflect the values of the Christian faith that it recognizes, and the Christian norms that have been established are ignored or flouted at large.

When, therefore, people within the society seek radical obedience to the values and norms of the Christian faith, there's a new process, a transformative or a constitutive process taking place that is quite properly called conversion. And so conversion in the West leads to radical Christian discipleship, and it becomes a recurrent feature of the Christian societies, the territorially Christian societies, that emerge from this Western process established by adoption of Christian symbols. Such conversions normally involve a personal crisis, sometimes a dramatic one, but once more they're related to expectations already formulated within the community. Usually they have, or at least lead to, a communal expression.

The archetypal story goes back before the conversion of the West. It goes back to Antony (d. 356), whom I have described as the first evangelical, though it would take too long to explain why. The whole point of Antony's conversion is that the society that he rejects is a Christian society. The state establishment of Christianity still lies far in the future, but in the lower Egypt of his day, Christianity is the accepted and acceptable religion. In other words, it has become possible to combine Christianity and self-indulgence in a way that was unthinkable in Justin's time. Antony is a well-off Christian.

His conversion takes place through hearing the Scriptures read in church. The particular passage is the story of the rich young ruler, who wanted to follow Christ but sorrowfully abandoned the idea on finding that it involved getting rid of his substantial possessions. Antony got rid of his own, by stages moved further and further into the desert. He wasn't allowed to be solitary. Others, stirred by the same thought of the gap between the Christian affirmations of what society should be and the actual practice of Christians, followed him there.

Antony represents the quest for radical obedience to Christian norms, which are established but not attained or even vigorously pursued in his own society. It's the beginning of the truly Christian community within the total Christian community. It recalls the remnant in Israel that meant the group within who maintain the true life of Israel, whose general corporate life denies it.

As territorial Christianity spread across northern Europe, it was manifest that to live the life of radical obedience within the normal demands and constraints of a violent society was difficult, perhaps impossible. The establishment of the monastic orders was an attempt to set up an alternative society where it would be possible to live a consistent Christian life. When Anselm—whom we've already met, the twelfth-century archbishop of Canterbury—was asked if many would be saved, he replied, "No. And most of those will be monks." Anselm lived in a Christian kingdom, but his appointment as archbishop of Canterbury involved life as a landlord, and it involved attendance at the king's court. He found both traumatic. Here is his pupil writing about him:

> He saw his days and nights taken up with secular business. He saw himself unable to devote his attention either to God or to his neighbor in God's name as he had formerly done. And he saw no one willing to listen to the word of life from his lips or to carry it out and thereby lost, he thought, his reward. He begins to doubt his salvation.
>
> To add to these evils of his own, a cruel oppression of his men daily afflicted his ears. *[He's a landlord, and he's got to leave his estates in the charge of stewards.]* He was deafened by the threats of worse to follow made by

malicious men. God knows how often I heard him most
vehemently protest that he'd rather be one of the boys in
the monastic community trembling under the master's
rod than sit aloft on the pontifical throne among the
congregation of the people, having the pastoral care of
the whole of Britain.

Just so in early times Jewish believers entered restored through
Jesus the Messiah, implicitly recognizing by baptism that
ethnic Jewishness was not enough, that though born in Israel
they were the moral equivalent of Gentile outsiders, so the
monasteries reflected the community seeking Christ's way within
Christendom. The way of the inner community was meant to
actualize what the whole community was in principle.

Not surprisingly, the decision by which one is led to entry
into a community truly devoted to the service of God is often
described as conversion. When Thomas à Kempis in *The
Imitation of Christ* talks about, "Remember your conversion,"
he means remember the time when you entered the monastery.
In the Middle Ages monks who turned from the world when
they were adults are distinguished from those who have been
offered as infants and brought up in the monastery.

Turning from the world, even if that is a world that nominally
recognizes the kingship of Christ, marks a turning from the
worldly self-centered life. For several centuries the only books of
devotion in the West were written for use in monasteries, for the
monastic life was the only way of devotion known.

Monastic history, and I needn't enlarge on this, showed
that radical obedience to the Christian norms cannot be
institutionalized. Abuses followed, scandalous abuses, and
the northern vernacular forms of Christianity that formed

Protestantism abandoned the monasteries and sought to bring the holy life back into the mainstream of Western social life. As Luther says, "A married cobbler can live as holy a life as a celibate monk."

But Protestantism in general continued the territorial principle of Christianity. It was soon clear that merely reforming the institutions and formularies of a Christian nation—even if, as in Geneva and elsewhere, godly discipline was applied to it— did not turn those nations into apostolic churches.

The radical wing of Protestantism, the so-called Anabaptist movement, was prepared to seek realization of the apostolic community by abandoning the territorial principle that had marked Western Christianity since its adoption by the northern peoples. True churches were companies of true believers. In effect, they continued the tradition of the monasteries. The gathered congregation is the Protestant version of the monastery—whole families of men, women, and children committed to the service of God. Northern Europe, I suspect, never really abolished the monasteries. They simply became Baptists and Mennonites.

We could take the story further to the development of evangelical conversion in the seventeenth and eighteenth centuries. It's too well known a phenomenon. But let me note two features of it. First, it matches the newly developing Western consciousness in those centuries of individuality. Thus, it gives a Christian expression to that individuality. In this respect evangelicalism is an indigenizing development in the West, helping to adjust Christianity to the modern world.

The second is that evangelical Christianity is a reflection of Christendom. It is a protest against a society that claims to be Christian but does not understand the nature of Christianity.

It posits a distinction between real or inward Christianity, and formal or nominal Christianity. It implies, that is, a Christian civil society.

This brings us back to that fundamental basis of Western Christianity, the idea of Christendom. We've seen that territorial Christianity arose from the nature of the primal cultures of the north. But it also transcended these cultures in a variety of ways. One of the most important and far reaching in its effects was the introduction of an element arising out of the Christian past in the Roman imperial world.

This was the idea of universality, of catholicity, transcending the various kinship groups and tributary relationships. In the West this was particularly potent by virtue of the special position of Rome, because Rome was the only assured link the West had with the apostolic age. In a sense the church continued the Roman Empire. If Rome had lost the imperial, political significance, it was still the seat of the empire of Christ, even when a holy Roman emperor sat somewhere else.

The role of the Christian church in maintaining and transmitting the cultural legacy of Rome strengthened the conception. In entering the Christian faith the peoples of the north and west entered a wider universe, recognized wider kinships than they had ever done before—a single assembly of Christian princes and peoples, a single church, a single sacred language, a single tradition of learning.

Anyone who could read, whether in Ireland, France, Hungary, or Poland, could read the same books in the same language. A single civilization fused elements from the Celtic and Germanic cultures with what it could absorb from the Roman Empire and preserved that empire's language, Latin, for purposes of learning and wider communication long after Latin had ceased to be anyone's vernacular. To be Christian was to share a special history and literary tradition, as it were by adoption. It was to be a late Roman. It was to belong also to specific territory, to Christian lands, the entire contiguous lands from Ireland to the Carpathians, states and peoples subject to princes who were subject to Christ, hearing the voice of Christ's apostle from the Eternal City that antedated them all.

English has two words, *Christianity*—which suggests a concept, a religious system, a term that you can use as a formal parallel for Hinduism or Buddhism—and *Christendom*, suggesting an entity with territorial and temporal dimensions, something that can be plotted on a map. Many European languages have only one word for both. The Christendom idea, the territorial principle of Christianity latched to the idea of a single inherited civilization, was brought into Christian history by the barbarian model of Christianity, much as the Hellenistic model of Christianity introduced the idea of orthodoxy.

Both were the natural outcome of the interaction of Christian faith and tradition with dominant cultural norms. The Christendom idea has been extraordinarily resilient. It survived the sixteenth-century Reformation practically unscathed. The Protestant Reformation resulted in the division of Christendom but not in the abandonment of the idea. The Protestant reformers held to it as firmly as any Catholic. What they sought was a reformed Christendom. They didn't recognize the possibility of opting out of the Reformed community. As in the Latin church, the Christian prince or magistrate had his proper duty. He stood in the place of Hezekiah or Josiah, the royal reformers of old Judah.

There were certainly more radical reformers, such as we've seen in the Anabaptist tradition, whose theology did undermine the Christendom concept. Their persecution by Catholic and Protestant alike shows how seriously that threat was taken. Yet when the radical reformers came to New England, they couldn't resist, at least for a brief period, setting up Christendom all over again, a pure and godly commonwealth uncorrupted by the tired old iniquities of Europe.

Let us consider Europe in 1500 or thereabouts. It's a supremely confident time for Christendom. The last pagan peoples of Europe in Finland and the Baltic States have been brought within Latin Christendom. Still more strikingly, Muslim power has been broken in sovereign Spain. The Muslims after centuries of presence there have been driven out or forced to accept incorporation into the church. Christianity can be described as virtually complete in its theology. It looks as though every important question has been canvassed and settled.

There's a secure tradition of literature, a flourishing tradition of art, and both owe their canons to the Bible and the church. It is sacred art that sets the artistic norms. It's sacred art—even though there is a secular art—that provides the register of symbols and conventions. Just at this point of self-assurance Europe came—by means of the expansion of the Iberian powers, Spain and Portugal—into massive contact with the non-Western world. With Christianity essentially territorial in concept, all recent experience pointed to crusade as the natural mode of relationship with that world.

The earliest colonialism was conceived in crusading. As early as 1415 the Portuguese conquered part of Morocco, a blow for Christendom against Islam. You may note in passing that the principal experience Western Europe had of the world beyond Christendom was of the Islamic world, which of course had a similar idea of relating faith to territory. You were either Dar al-Islam or Dar al-Harb.

A passage in a near contemporary account about Prince Henry the Navigator of Portugal tells how he wrote to all the kings of Christendom inviting their help in discovery and conquest for the service of our Lord on the basis of shared profits. They all sent apologies for absence, which Henry collected and sent to the pope. This response was exactly what he wanted and was formalized in the course of the next century or so in the Madurado Patronato, by which the pope not only gave to the monarchs of Portugal and Spain monopoly powers of trade and rule in the worlds that they were now meeting, but committed to them the oversight of the church in those lands. This last point, I think, represents the first reflex action of colonialism on Christendom and perhaps the first step in the secularization of Western society.

The Iberian voyagers, with the French and the Dutch and the English ones who followed, and their resulting settlements and conquest altered the map of European and of Christian knowledge. The British scholar J. H. Elliott has pointed out that the maps and the reference books did not immediately alter. It took contemporaries some time to take in the new discoveries. It's often the way. Discoveries that remove the old landmarks and undermine the accepted concepts of the world are ignored for as long as possible.

The natural objective was to incorporate these new lands within Christendom. The only known model of Christianity was territorial, and the precedent of crusade so recently blessed with prosperity and the restoration of Granada to the rule of Christ seemed to authorize the use of the sword to bring about its extension. Conversion would be the fruit of conquest.

At first it seemed to work. In Mexico, in Peru, and in the Philippines the Spaniards destroyed indigenous cults, proscribed traditional rites, and baptized whole populations. It was not long, however, before the difficulty such methods created were apparent. A century after the conquest one earnest priest is lamenting that because of the work of destruction he knows so little of the old culture, and because of his ignorance. "They can practice idolatry before my very eyes. I don't know when they're doing it!"

Such an utterance marks the beginning of self-doubt. Destruction of cult was easy. Trying to comprehend a society so different from the norm of Christendom exposed the gaps in European intellectual equipment and before long exposed the gaps in its theology too. The only tools at hand for understanding the non-Christian world lay in the pre-Christian Latin classics. The only pagans European Christians knew anything about were to be met there. Ovid and Virgil were, in fact, not much use for understanding Quechua or Aymara society.

The issue was of no great moment from a strictly colonial point of view. It might be urged that understanding wasn't formerly necessary. It was enough to compel. But as the heart cry of the priest already quoted indicates, this compulsion breaks down at the pastoral level. Similarly, from a colonial point of view the use of indigenous language isn't an issue. The Spanish language of the conquerors can be imposed, and from the point of view of European theologians this is welcome. The European controversies of the sixteenth century had set a premium on accurate definition. A range of doctrines and liturgical practices was being more precisely formulated than ever before, and all those official formulations were in Latin.

But for pastoral practice this wasn't much help. How could an Andean peasant make confession to salvation if he didn't understand? The only way forward was to grapple with understanding the Andean vernaculars and attempt to explain Christian doctrine in indigenous terms. Europe-based theologians and the local guardians of colonial safety in church and state both took fright in this. The Andean languages did not have, they said, the words or the concepts to safeguard saving truth. Or they were so riddled with false concepts of the divine as to make their use dangerous.

European experience also suggested that there was a close link between vernacular translation and heresy. Official policy thus suggested using borrowed words from Latin or Spanish for all-important concepts. But the use of borrowed words, of course, solved nothing. If confession is to be made from the heart, the borrowed words have to be understood in the vernacular. In fact, a two-way traffic was being set up between Christian theology and the Andean worldview as early as this, and ideas were being apprehended in terms of ideas that were already in the Andes. As William Mitchell puts it, "The option for the vernacular means that no one can speak of the Christianization of the Andes in the early colonial period unless one speaks of the Andeanization of Christianity."

Meanwhile the brutality and rapacity of the representatives of Christendom taken as a whole called into question the moral and thus the Christian status of the Spanish mission. The story of Bartolomé de las Casas and in particular his passionate debates with Sepúlveda show how the affairs of America forced new questions onto the theological agenda—questions about the constitution of humanity and about the place of compulsion in religion, about the conditions of the just war.

Already America was showing the limitations of Western theology, of that assured encyclopedia that had been built up over the centuries of Christian Europe. An observer attentive to the issues facing the missionaries in Mexico or Peru, even those arising out of the catechism itself, easily concluded that the task of theology was not complete. The wider question of the extent to which Andean Christianity was developing a life of its own didn't become apparent until the present century.

The success of the Spanish project to incorporate its new world into Christendom was thus more apparent than real. However, much more important for the future of Christendom than the apparent success of the Spanish was the fact that the Portuguese found it well-nigh impossible. The Spanish presence was concentrated in America and the Philippines. The Portuguese were stretched like a thread along the coasts of Africa, the Persian Gulf, across the Indian Ocean, into South India, Sri Lanka, along the coasts and islands of southeast Asia, on to offshore China, onward to Japan—not to mention, of course, Brazil.

Much of this area was not so much an empire as a system of trade monopolies staffed by little companies of merchants, soldiers, and priests. And Portugal was a small country with a standing army never above ten thousand men. Portugal began her empire with joyful acceptance of the task of expanding Christendom, but her resources were slender, her hold often precarious, and even in the territories, the small territories that she occupied, Islam, Hinduism, and Buddhism refused to lie down. The result was important for Christianity.

It was in the Portuguese territories and still more in the powerful states on which the Portuguese presence in India and China depended that the conditions appeared that called forth the modern missionary movement. In the Spanish territories the task was to teach the faith to people already obliged to receive it. The Portuguese experience allowed only limited scope for this. The Portuguese experience did, however, make necessary the creation of a new body of people who did not have the power of coercion, whose function was to commend, to persuade, to demonstrate, and to discuss, and who in order to perform these tasks needed to understand the life of other societies.

The original conception of the expansion of Christendom involved laying down terms for other people. Its new development in the missionary movement involved preparedness to live on terms set by other people. It was initially by invitation that the Jesuits arrived at the court of the Mughal emperor Akbar the Great. The arrival at the court of the Chinese emperor Tang relied on perseverance. Once there, in either case, their ways of working were circumscribed by the interests of those monarchs. They had to conduct themselves in accordance with local custom and find a niche within local society.

Some sought a high degree of identification and cultural transfer, the most famous early example being Roberto de Nobili with his adoption of the lifestyle of a Brahman Sannyasi and his refusal to be classed as Portuguese, the only locally known form of European. Sometimes the approach to another culture was less dramatic but equally remarkable in its cultural achievement. The missionary Giuseppe Beschi, for instance, is a seminal figure in Tamil literature. In this strange way, interfaith dialogue was born of frustrated colonialism. Putting it another way, in the mercy of God the king of Portugal never had enough servants to go out into the highways and byways and compel them to come in.

The fundamental missionary experience is to live on terms set by others. This was true in a literal sense for a high proportion of the missionaries between the middle of the sixteenth century and the middle of the nineteenth, who were subject to conditions laid down by the sovereign rulers of the territories in which they lived, or were able to carry on their missionary work only because the leaders of that society found them useful for something else.

The colonial advance, of course, and especially the high imperial period between 1880 and 1920 altered a great deal of this by creating another power structure. Even with these conditions, however, missionaries as a class, not always by their own desire, had to take note of others' terms more than most Europeans of the colonial period. The need to speak someone else's language; the consciousness of doing it badly, perhaps laughably badly; being unsure of etiquette; constantly afraid of giving unintended offense; realizing more and more the vast depth and complexity of another community's traditions and history and thus its identity: all this was part of the daily experience of thousands. It led to some herculean efforts of understanding and sympathy and to the collection and systemization of knowledge.

Their primary aim was to enter the hearts and minds of other people, since that was the only effective way they could talk about Christ. In the process they altered the map of Western learning more than any other group of Western residents in the non-Western world. If some of the results now seem absurd or offensive, it may be well to remember that we're all subject to the principle that it is not possible to take in a new idea except in the terms of an idea we already have.

Perhaps part of the significance of the missionary movement is the very converse of the cultural imperialism with which it's often quite justifiably charged. The missionary movement arose from the need to live on someone else's terms, to make Christian affirmations within the constraints of someone else's language. The missionary movement is the learning experience of Western Christianity. It's more, because in the process of introducing Christian affirmations in other languages it set them free to move within new systems of thought and discourse.

Lamin Sanneh has shown us how in many parts of Africa missionary activity acted as a means of cultural renewal by its use of vernaculars and, in the production of vernacular worshiping communities and the creation of vernacular literatures, hymnody, and liturgy, provided resistance to eroding influences from outside. He draws attention to the fact that his own Mandinka people, who have been Muslim for centuries, have forgotten their own name for God, whereas in almost all areas of West Africa where Christian influences predominated, the God and Father of the Lord Jesus Christ has a vernacular name.

The Western theological process starts from the fact that the northern and western barbarians abandoned their old pantheons and took in God from the outside, envisaged in terms of Yahweh of Hosts, the God of Israel, merged with the highest good of the Greek philosophical tradition. African theology starts at a different point: God has a vernacular name. As Olorun, as Nyame, as Ngewo, He is there in the African, indeed in the Yoruba, the Akamba, the Mende past. From one point of view the Western missionary movement can be seen as the last flourish of Christendom. From another it represents a departure from Christendom, perhaps an Abrahamic journey out of it.

The missionary movement had another effect on Christendom, not envisaged in its origins. The establishment of a body of European Christians, working however inconsistently on a different set of terms from the official colonial presence, gradually introduced a principle of separation between the religion of Christendom and its political, military, and economic power. The wedge was narrow to begin with, but it's there visible in de Nobili's vigorous rejection of the Portuguese name and in the demeanor and activities of many other early missionaries who did not come from the lands that held Padroado.

The later colonialisms witnessed a thickening of the wedge. The Dutch, who succeeded the Portuguese in so much of their empire, maintained the Portuguese religious policy, simply substituting reform for Catholic worship. But they had no missionary orders. And the predicants of the trading companies were limited in their effect on communities outside the church. The Honorable East India Company, the mode of British administration in India down to 1858, for a long time ostentatiously dissociated itself from Christianity and, even after 1813 when evangelical pressure in Parliament secured the insertion of pious clauses into its charter, maintained a more than discreet distance.

Missionaries, Protestant or Catholic, had grown up in Christendom and, taken as a group, had no quarrel with it. The first evangelical missionary project for British India envisaged what would have been in effect a state mission. What better gift could Britain give to the territories over whom Providence had set it than the gospel of Christ? What greater treason could it commit than to hide that gospel? Even after the cataclysm of 1857 (the year of the "Indian Mutiny"), evangelicals were demanding that Britain identify itself in India as the Christian nation it was. "Britain is the first conqueror of India," said Lord Shaftsbury, "who has not let it be known what his religion is." But they spoke in vain, and great was their scandal to find the British government the official guardian by treaty of the Temple of the Tooth in Kandy and legally responsible for the appointment of Buddhist priests.

Catholic missionary spokesmen fared no better. Cardinal Charles Lavigerie saw in Algeria the possibility of an Arab Catholic peasantry that would be the mirror image of Brittany. But the French government legislated against the conversion of Muslims and was prepared to prosecute any who tried.

By the end of the nineteenth century there is a clear note of embattlement in missionary literature, a sense of betrayal by the Christians of the state. At the beginning of the nineteenth century the great Islamic power had been the sultan of Turkey.

By the end it was the British Empire, with the Royal Republic of the Netherlands in second place. The missionary interest was lamenting that Britain kept missionaries out of the emirates of Northern Nigeria and was encouraging the Islamization of the Sudan. And furthermore the British did these things more efficiently than the sultan of Turkey had ever done. In the twentieth century it appeared that the most considerable religious effects of imperial rule were the renovation and reformulation of a Hinduism that had seemed to be disintegrating when British rule was first established and a quite unprecedented spread of Islam. Colonial rule did more for Islam in Africa than all the jihads put together.

Colonialism, in fact, helped to transform the Christian position in the world by forcing a distinction between Christianity and Christendom. Colonial experience undermined the identification of Christianity and territory and immobilized the idea of crusade. It introduced new theological and moral questions, for the issues argued in one century by las Casas, in another by T. F. Buxton and John Philip, go to the heart of religion. Fundamentally their questions are about salvation. It opened the way for a Christian understanding and interpretation of other religions and cultures for which the conditions of Western Christianity provided no space. It undermined that pillar of Christendom, church establishment, because the principles of establishment could hardly ever be maintained abroad.

It is usual and entirely correct in describing the colonial period to point to connections between the Christian missionaries and the colonial states. Perhaps the reverse, however, is equally true. It's the colonial period that marks the divergence of interest between Christianity and the Western powers, the separation of the religion of the West from its economic and political interests. If several generations of missionaries once felt betrayed when a state that was nominally Christian refused to offer them the support which they felt they were due, we may now be humbly grateful that God is often kinder than to answer all the prayers of His people.

Paradoxically and in sharp contrast to its first vision, colonialism helped to ensure that new Christendoms did not arise. The pattern of that colonial rule prevented the development of the relationship of throne and altar that had developed in the northern lands. In sub-Saharan Africa, the most remarkable theater of Christian accession in the modern world where it would be easy to draw African parallels in this century and the last to the stories from Gregory and Bede with which we began, the conversions have not had the same issue. And the fact that they did not is at least in part due to colonialism. Colonial rule brought together diverse peoples of different religious affiliation in units dictated by administrative convenience. The present states of sub-Saharan Africa are virtually all colonial constructs, based on colonial frontiers, which makes them of their nature religiously as well as ethnically plural, a natural home of the secular state.

The new chapter of Christianity, therefore, seems to relate to a Christianity without Christendom, a Christianity more and more determined by the sovereign continents. But perhaps the most striking single feature of Christianity today is the fact that the church now looks more like "that great multitude whom no man can number," drawn from all tribes and kindreds and people and tongues, than ever before in its history. Its diversity and its history lead to a great variety of starting points for its theology. It reflects varying bodies of experience. The study of history and theology from this period on will increasingly need to operate from the position where most Christians are, and that will be the continents of Africa, Asia, Latin America, and the Pacific. Shared reading of the Scriptures and shared theological reflection will be to the benefit of all, but the oxygen-deprived West will have the most to gain.

Encounters

CHAPTER 5

Worldviews and Christian Conversion

Worldviews are the mental maps of the universe that contain what we know, or think we know, about it and how it works, and about our own place in it. We use these maps to navigate a way through the universe. We compile them from many sources: from our own observation and experience, from our family and education, from the outlook and customs of our community, from the accumulation of sources we believe we have reason to trust. For certain purposes, we may borrow a map from a source that we do not regularly use, rather as one might consult an atlas for a specialized point. For instance, we may consult, but only occasionally, the "atlas" of the religious system to which we give general allegiance or recognition. In such cases we copy additional detail from the atlas on to our own operating map. We are unlikely to copy all the maps that we find in the atlas of the religious system; while some points will seem crucial, others will appear unimportant, some perhaps not comprehensible. The crucial items we will copy on to our own map in detail; those that seem less important to us in sketchy outline.

The maps will cover not only the phenomenal world of what we can see and touch, but whatever we recognize as transcending that world, what we might call the sphere of religion. They will contain our ideas of morality and of obligation, the rights and duties that we recognize. They contain our sense of relationships, family and kin, clan and nation; to whom we belong and why, to whom we do not belong and why. They include our views of society with its ranks and hierarchies, and they indicate where we see our place in them. The maps also show what we see as places of safety where we may walk with confidence, and areas of danger, where we walk warily or not at all.

The maps indicate the degree of contingency we feel, the degree of certainty and predictability that we take to be normal, the degree of recognition we give to the activity of forces beyond our control. In this matter, maps vary greatly. In so-called modern worldviews the contingency factor is low; people expect to be in general control of their environment, the electric light to come on at the pressing of a switch, clean water to come from turning a tap. By contrast, much of humanity, in earlier times and today, lives with a high degree of contingency, conscious of dependence on the uncontrollable, not only for light and clean water but for the daily food supply. The maps will also indicate places of power, support, and protection; and the larger the places of danger are marked on the map, and the higher the degree of contingency, the larger these places of power and protection, and the ways to them, will be plotted also.

For all these elements are plotted on the worldview map in relation to each other. One aspect of this are the connecting pathways, rather like roads on a geographical map, that link, for instance, the rights and duties area both to the religion area and the kin relationships areas, and the places of danger to the sources of power and protection. Another is that the elements are plotted on the worldview map according to their relative sizes in operational importance.

It is important to distinguish conceptual from operational importance. Many peoples, for instance, have a God component on their worldview maps, and believe God to be supreme, the creator and moral governor of the universe. These are huge concepts, and on a conceptual map would be represented very large. But worldview maps are operational; and in the operational religion of many peoples who have such concepts of God, far more attention is paid to territorial divinities who control the land, or to ancestors who maintain the family and the clan, or to intermediary beings of some kind than to God. On their worldview maps, therefore, God appears relatively small, the other entities significantly larger.

Nor is this a feature of the worldviews only of so-called primal societies. We have already noted that worldview maps make selective use of the "atlases" of the great religious systems, copying in detail from the constituent maps features that appear crucial for operational purposes, sketching others in broader outline, ignoring others altogether. This process occurs among Christians, Muslims, and Buddhists alike—and in the construction of an infinite number of personal worldview maps.

For worldview maps are both personal and collective, the collective being identifiable where a community shares the same trusted sources, and thus makes use of broadly similar elements in broadly similar relationships. There may be oscillation and variation caused by some members of the community using trusted sources that other members do not. In this connection we may note that, except as an abstract concept, there is no such thing as the Christian worldview. There are elements from the sources that Christians in general trust, which will give a broad similarity to their operational maps; but Christians from any given place or time will have other sources that they share, not with their fellow-Christians of other cultures, but with the non-Christians of their own. There are, in practice, various Christian worldviews, all sharing Christian elements, but some sharing other operational features with Muslim or Buddhist or primal traditionalist or modern agnostic neighbors.

With this in mind, we can proceed to consider how worldviews change.

Changing Worldviews

Worldviews, and the operational mapping process that produces them, are subject to change. They can be influenced by new ideas, outside events, emotional upheavals, the expansion of knowledge. Rarely, however, are worldviews entirely destroyed and replaced by completely different ones. What usually happens is that people modify their maps of reality, adding the new information correcting ideas they now see as wrong, altering the relationship of one set of ideas to another, making some bigger, some smaller, crossing some out altogether. It is a process analogous to the way geographical maps are constructed and updated: marking on an old map a town that was not known to us before, or altering the shape of a stretch of coastline to indicate a bay or an inlet imperfectly explored previously, or showing a new road while deleting an old one no longer in use. Very rarely do people throw away the map altogether. Worldview maps, human operational systems, are usually revised and corrected, not abandoned and replaced.

It is important to remember this in relation to Christian conversion and to Christian nurture. We must not use New Testament passages that describe the new creation in Christ[1] and

---

[1] E.g., 2 Corinthians 5:17.

the moral renewal brought by the Holy Spirit as though they left no continuity with the past. Just as God made Adam from the dust of the earth and breathed into him the breath of life,[2] so the new creation takes place with preexisting materials. We are made by our past; it is our past that has shaped our identity; it is on the basis of the past that our operational maps have been constructed and are now open to revision. Our past cannot be abandoned; we cannot immediately draw a new map from scratch. Our past cannot be substituted by someone else's past, like Gentile proselytes entering old Israel; nor can it be left as it is. The past has to be converted. In its simplest sense, conversion means turning—turning what is already there toward Christ. It is less about content than about direction.

When people become Christians, they do not throw away their maps of reality; the new elements are placed on the old maps. The old maps are modified to include new information, to delete wrong or outdated information, to alter the proportions of one element to another, as some components get bigger and some smaller. If God was on the map of reality before, that part of the map will almost certainly expand. Perhaps becoming Christian will mean that Christ is plotted on the operational map for the first time. But while some elements on the map may change drastically, others will change little, or not at all. For instance, Christian conversion may be slow to produce any major alteration in the ideas of relationship and belonging; the first changes in this area will probably bring recognition of kinship with other Christians belonging to communities other than the one constituted by biological kinship. Conversion may not alter the safe and dangerous places that are marked on the map; the latter especially may remain exactly as they were before. Beliefs about

---

[2] Genesis 2:7.

witchcraft and sorcery may be in exactly the same place on the mental map of the universe as before, even if there is now a more intense unwillingness actually to employ sorcery than previously.

People who become Christians do not throw away a worldview called "primal" or "Muslim" or "Buddhist" and take a new one called "Christian"; they amend their maps of reality to include new information and correct what they now see as errors. The new Christian elements will be placed on the old map; and elements that seem characteristically "primal," or "Muslim," or "Buddhist" may still be on the operational map—and not necessarily in operational conflict with the Christian elements. Christian conversion involves turning what is already there— primal things, Islamic things, Buddhist things—toward Christ.

So Christians whose worldview has been shaped by one culture will have a somewhat different operational map of reality from Christians whose worldview has been shaped by another culture. There is no one single Christian worldview. There are Christian worldviews sharing vital elements, and these shared elements bring them close together and make them quite different from non-Christian worldviews from the same culture; but they may still be sharply differentiated from each other. Christian worldviews may have important elements in common with non-Christian worldviews of the cultures from which they come—features that will differ from those on the worldview maps of their fellow Christians of another cultural background.

Christian ideas commonly penetrate deeper with Christian teaching; that is, theology is introduced from the Christian atlas, and more information is added to the mental map. But there may still seem no reason to alter the area on the map where safe and dangerous places are marked. Beliefs about witchcraft and sorcery may remain very much the same. On the other hand, the sources of power and protection may have been completely revised: the old protective mechanisms against evil have been deleted; statements from the theological atlas about Christ as the source of power and protection are now on the map. But previously there was a pathway marked on the map that linked the place of danger to the source of protection. With the deletion of the old source of protection, that path has now disappeared from the map, and there is no clear pathway from the (still clearly marked) concrete danger of witchcraft to the theological statement about the love and power of Christ.

Early in the twentieth century, Donald Fraser, a sensitive Scottish missionary in what is now Malawi, described a common type of experience in the church in Livingstonia, where the mission schools and hospital were often held up as a model.[3] A young woman, a church member, has dreadful complications in the later stages of pregnancy. Why should this happen? There must be a reason. She knows she has been faithful, and begins to wonder if the cause lies in her husband's misbehavior. He, sure of his own innocence, begins to wonder about his wife's. Family and neighbors differ in their guesses as to who is to blame. Those prepared to swear by the innocence of both parties suspect witchcraft or sorcery—and begin to calculate who among their acquaintances might have an interest in causing mischief, and thus employed the psychic powers of witchcraft or the spiritual technology of sorcery. The woman is attending the antenatal clinic at the mission hospital. Her condition is identified, a healthy baby is triumphantly delivered in the hospital, the mother is safe, the church receives both and thanks God.

---

[3] See Donald Fraser, *African Idylls: Portraits and Impressions of Life on a Central African Mission Station* (London: Seeley, Service, 1923). On Fraser, see T. Jack Thompson, *Christianity in Northern Malawi: Donald Fraser's Missionary Methods and Ngoni Culture* (Leiden: Brill, 1995).

And there, typically, the account in the missionary magazine will end. But Fraser was aware that the story does not end there. Everyone remembers that something went wrong in the first place, and there must have been a reason for this. Husband and wife continue to have a niggling doubt at the back of their minds over what the other did, and there is a shadow over trust that no triumph of modern medicine can drive away. The relatives continue to speculate about the part played by the putative secret enemy, and add this to the grievances they already have against the person they have identified as that enemy. And Fraser, writing in the 1920s, admits that at present there was nothing in the church's armory that could cope with this situation.

The problem is not a matter of faith: these are sincere, believing Christians. Nor is there anything wrong with the teaching they have received. The problem lies in the gap between the teaching and the mental maps of the universe. Our deepest operational beliefs are not necessarily those we state, but those we think we have no need to state—because we take them to be universal. And everyone in Livingstonia "knew" that a whole network of spiritual forces of diverse origin, some of them open to manipulation, were at work in the world. They also knew that in the way the world is constituted, moral (and for that matter ritual) misbehavior will reap its own reward. Complications in pregnancy could never be assumed to be a medical matter alone.

Missions and Modern Worldviews

Between the young couple and the mission hospital lies the Enlightenment. For several centuries European Christians used maps of the universe in which Christian elements dominated. These included the theme of One God who created the world, redeemed it through the sacrifice of Christ, and in the end would judge all humanity. But those maps still marked certain danger areas in the way that the pre-Christian European maps did. Witchcraft, for instance, was thought of as desperately dangerous as it always had been before Christianity came to Europe. On Christian maps, witchcraft remained, therefore. Indeed, it now had a theological explanation that it had not before; witches were people who had made a pact with the devil, and in European Christian countries witchcraft was a criminal offense, punishable by death, often by burning, to symbolize how important it was to destroy all trace of witchcraft completely.

Similarly European Christians continued to believe in supernatural interventions; just as evil such as witchcraft was attributed to the Devil, so interventions for good were attributed to God. For centuries prayers to saints were held to produce miraculous healings; special holy places were charged with supernatural powers to help. In Protestant Europe this died down, because there was no place left for prayer to saints; but in Catholic Europe the idea of miracles continued.

In the seventeenth and eighteenth centuries a series of intellectual movements took place in different parts of Europe. Collectively these are now known as the Enlightenment, a word suggesting illumination by the new knowledge of what had been the darkness of ignorance. Enlightenment took many forms, but some important elements were the exaltation of reason, the development of science, and the heightening of the sense of autonomy of the individual self.

Christian Europe had taken for granted a foundation of revelation. Protestant Christians tended to identify revelation with the Bible, Catholic Christians with the authority of the church. Enlightenment principles challenged both. There is a strong argument for linking science with the Protestant Reformation, but the Enlightenment gave it a major boost.

Science demanded a uniform universe where the same process repeated under the same conditions produces the same result—laws of nature mean that the world works in a uniform way every time. But miracles represent a breach of natural order and cannot be repeated. As for the autonomy of the self, Descartes set out the principle "I think therefore I exist"—that is, the individual is defined by his own mental activity, not by membership of a community. But Europe had long defined itself as a Christian community, indeed, as *the* Christian community, Christendom. People were Christians because they were born in a Christian country; they were baptized in infancy since they had been born into the sphere of salvation; they lived under Christian laws from which they could not opt out. If Descartes was right, all this must be wrong. Religion belonged rather to the sphere of private judgment.

So the Enlightenment posed a challenge to the traditional Christian worldview at key points: the primacy of reason in relation to revelation, the uniform laws of nature in relation to divine intervention through miracles, individual autonomy in relation to the corporate identification with territorial Christendom.

Through the Enlightenment Christianity lost some ground in Europe, but, at least at first, less than might have been expected. Certainly there was a stream of Enlightenment thinking that was hostile to Christianity, and that stream began the secularization of Europe. But on the whole Christianity adjusted to Enlightenment thinking, and Christian worldviews were modified to reflect both Enlightenment and Christian ideas. Hence there are both Christian and non-Christian Enlightenment worldviews. What they had in common was a firm distinction between natural and supernatural. They posit a "natural" world roughly corresponding to what one can see and touch, where natural laws operate uniformly and the principle of repeatability can be used to verify statements. This natural or empirical world has a firm boundary. On the other side of that boundary with the natural world lies what one might call the world of spirit, the transcendent world. Many non-Christian Enlightenment thinkers said in effect that the spirit world does not exist, or if it does, we can know nothing about it. Christian thinkers insisted that the other side of the frontier was real and that God did intervene in the empirical to reveal Himself. Revelation occurred at defined crossing places on the frontier. In practice Christian Enlightenment thinkers held that these frontier crossings were limited. They argued, for instance, that miracles were a special dispensation belonging to the time of Christ and His apostles, and had now ceased. Likewise, dreams and visions belonged to biblical times; they were not reliable guides to the transcendent world now. Dreams, indeed, usually had a physical or psychological basis. In these days guidance should come from Scripture and reason, informed of course by prayer; healing by means of scientific medicine, that is, by applying consecrated reason to the world that God had created. And witchcraft—that was a delusion. It was impossible to manipulate the natural world except in accordance with natural laws. The burning of witches had been a horrible mistake, cruel persecution of vulnerable or emotionally disturbed people. And so, witchcraft ceased to be a criminal offense and disappeared from the statute books of Europe.

The Enlightenment universe is the basis of "modern" worldviews. Enlightenment worldviews are maps of a universe smaller than that of most European Christians before the Enlightenment and smaller than those used by most people living in Africa or Asia. Christian and non-Christian Enlightenment worldviews had in common that they left no place for witchcraft or sorcery, those danger signs marked on so many worldview maps. Christians and non-Christians might dispute about whether miracles happened, but generally the dispute was over whether they had happened in the past; no one was expecting the laws of nature to be suspended now. This meant reading the Bible, especially the Old Testament but also some parts of the New Testament, in a certain way: recognizing that God had used frontier crossings in the past that since the time of the apostles had been closed. Christians were now to exercise their ministry according to the way God had created the world, "thinking God's thoughts after Him," as the great astronomer Kepler put it. So education and medicine were areas to which Christians were especially called.

In this type of worldview the existence of the demonic was problematic. Many non-Christian Enlightenment thinkers tended to ignore it, or to attribute evil to ignorance; more enlightenment would banish it. Christians clearly had to face the issue of evil; but now that they had accepted the autonomy of the self, they often tended to see evil in terms of individual guilt and sin. The phenomenon known as possession was, like most irrational behavior, perceived as a form of insanity.

All this meant putting brackets round parts of Scripture. The dreams, the visions, the healings, the prophecies, the works of power, belonged to an earlier stage of God's saving activity; such things had ceased with the apostolic age, and had little to do with contemporary Christian practice. They were genuine crossing places on the frontier between the transcendent and empirical worlds—but those crossing places were now boarded up.

Coping with the Enlightenment was not a matter of Christian retreat: it was a massive act of cultural adjustment, an act of contextualization. Nor did it fundamentally divide the more liberal from the more conservative Christians. It is hard to think of a more powerful advocate of a Christian Enlightenment world view than that staunch defender of biblical infallibility, B. B. Warfield.[4]

Enlightenment Christianity became the regular form in which the Christianity of the Protestant missionary movement was expressed. And the Enlightenment universe is the basis of modern Western theology, whether liberal or conservative.

The earliest Catholic missions took place before the Enlightenment; reading accounts of missions in the Congo in the sixteenth century, one senses much in common in the outlook of the Catholic missionaries and the Congolese people whom they met. Protestant missions did not start until the Enlightenment was well established, and it took firmer hold in Protestant Northern Europe than in Catholic Southern Europe. The missionary movement thus brings the Enlightenment with it. It brought education and healthcare. It brought modernity with the gospel.

Christian Preaching and
Traditional Maps of the Universe

Let us consider the worldviews of those hearing the gospel from Protestant missionaries with an Enlightenment worldview. Most of those societies had a larger, more populated universe than the modern one. Thus there were things on the worldview maps that no theology would fit, because the theology belonged to an Enlightenment modern universe and was thus too small to fit the larger universe of Africa.

Traditional African maps of the universe often had four components relating to the transcendent world: God,

---

[4] See B. B. Warfield, *Miracles, Yesterday and Today, True and False* (Grand Rapids: Eerdmans, 1965; originally published as *Counterfeit Miracles, 1918*).

local divinities or territorial spirits, ancestors, and objects of power. Traditional systems varied as to which of these was the dominating element, the biggest component on the map. In some systems God was the largest component, while in many others, it was the local divinities—people believed in God but their religious practice was dominated much more by attention to the divinities, the lesser divine beings. Others had ancestor-dominated systems, where consultation of ancestral spirits played a larger part than God or divinities. Not all systems had all four components; if Okot p'Bitek is correct, the central Luo have no God component on their maps;[5] whereas peoples such as the Gikuyu have neither local divinities nor, for purposes of religion, ancestral spirits.

All sorts of influences can modify the maps—dramatic or traumatic experiences for a people, religious influences from neighboring peoples or movements of reformation or renewal. Sometimes indigenous prophets have arisen and altered the relative position of components on the map. In the nineteenth century the prophet Mohlomi arose in Southern Africa among the Sotho, and influenced the great Sotho leader Moshoeshoe and his people. They had an ancestor-dominated system; under Mohlomi's influence they moved to a system dominated by the God of Heaven. It was not that they did not know about God before, but through the prophet movement the worship of God came to play a much greater part in Sotho life. In later years this helped to influence the Sotho toward Christianity, which almost invariably expands the God component on worldview maps; but in this case the expansion started well before the Sotho came into contact with Christianity. A similar event occurred in

---

[5] See Okot p'Bitek, *The Religion of the Central Luo* (Nairobi: East Africa Literature Bureau, 1971).

southern Ethiopia among the Wolayta in the 1930s and '40s, where a prophet movement shifted allegiance of some peoples from local divinities to the God of Heaven and prepared the way for a movement toward the Christian faith.[6]

Let us now consider the effect of Christian preaching on these traditional maps. If people respond at all to Christian preaching, they will add information to their map or alter the relative position of the components, expanding some, reducing some, perhaps erasing some. It is not likely that they will throw away the map altogether, replacing it by a totally new one. Many of the items will not move at all; there may seem, for instance, no reason to alter any of the perceptions about witchcraft or sorcery, especially among people who do not see themselves as witches or sorcerers. If dreams and visions were important before, they will continue to be so, but with a Christian content. If possession was important, it may continue in a new form, explained in biblical terms. Enlightenment maps, that is, modern maps of the universe, have a sharp line between the phenomenal or empirical world and the world of spirit. The new maps leave that frontier open and allow for frequent traffic between the spirit world and the phenomenal world. There is, in fact, much more detail on these maps than on the maps used by Western people. They reflect larger, more populated universes.

The element on the map that is first likely to show change and a Christian impact is the God element. The God element is present to some extent in a majority of maps; conceptually, but by no means always, operationally important. Under Christian impact, this often changes: the God element is magnified, expands over areas of the map that it did not cover before. God

---

[6] Paul Balisky, *Wolaiita Evangelists: A Study of Religion in Southern Ethiopia, 1937–1975* (Eugene, OR: Pickwick, 2009).

(usually known by a vernacular name) becomes invested with attributes from the Bible. We may note in passing that this is quite different from the European experience. In Europe, God did not have a vernacular name; no one said that Zeus or Jupiter or Odin was the father of our Lord Jesus Christ. In Europe, the One God was proclaimed over against the old gods, the One against the many. In Africa, the God of the Bible was generally identified with the God element already on the world map. God becomes bigger, nearer; He is the one to whom the believer is taught to go for power and protection.

The God element may expand into the space once occupied by the divinity element—the divinities who were either rulers of a particular locality or of a particular department of life. In the traditional system they received recognition, perhaps with shrine offerings. As people turn to the Christian faith, the conviction grows that honor belongs to God alone.

But the divinity component does not necessarily disappear from the map altogether. For one thing, when Christians find themselves in difficulty for which they can see no help in the Christian system, they may make some recognition of the divinities, not permanently, not putting them back into their old places on the map, but as a one-off or occasional resort. This fact probably reinforces a tendency, very evident within the charismatic movement in Africa, to see the divinities as demons. They are the rivals, and thus the enemies of God, spiritual entities with real existence, but essentially evil. In this case the divinities do not drop off the map. They take a new place on it as demonic forces.

But with the enlargement of the God component the divinities have sometimes been incorporated into African Christian maps in other ways. After all, are the divinities always to be seen as the rivals of God, and not as His servants? There have been many interpretations of African indigenous religions that see the divinities as agents, even as refractions of God (for instance, Idowu's interpretation of Yoruba belief in which the orisas are refractions of God's being[7]). Many people have argued that Africa has a different picture of the relations of God and the divinities from that reflected in the Semitic world of the Old Testament. In the Semitic world, the gods were rivals of Yahweh and must be rejected; in Africa, it is argued, the divinities are the servants of the God of Heaven.[8]

But who in Scripture are the spirit-servants of God but the angels? Some of the African Independent Churches or "spiritual" churches stress the ministry of angels; and they draw attention to the importance of angels, sometimes named angels, in some parts of the New Testament—parts bracketed out in a Enlightenment worldview. Does the stress on angelic ministry in these churches arise in partial compensation for the loss of the activity of the divinities in traditional religion? One feature of contemporary African Christianity is the opposition between the radical charismatics and the "spirituals," whom the former accuse of occult activity. Perhaps both groups are using the same maps of the spiritual world, maps drawn in pre-Christian Africa, and now revised in Christian response. They color the maps differently; perhaps what are colored as angels in one are colored as demons in the other. But neither map represents the Enlightenment version of the missionary period.

---

[7] E. Bolaji Idowu, *Olodumare: God in Yoruba Belief* (London: Longmans, 1962).

[8] P. J. Ryan, "'Arise, O God!' The Problem of 'Gods' in West Africa," *Journal of Religion in Africa* 11, no. 3 (1980): 161–71.

New Frontiers in Theology

We are in a period of theological ferment, when theological activity outside the West is needed to overcome major deficiencies in the Western theological tradition. Some of these arise from its long acculturation to a particular view of the world, not shared by the greater part of humanity. That worldview is now showing signs of losing its grip on the West itself. It is not that Western theology is wrong; simply that it is too small for the operating systems of Africa and, indeed, of most of the world. A vast expansion of theological activity is needed as the interaction of the Christian faith with the cultures—the operating systems—of Africa and Asia throw up new issues for theology. Christian interaction with Hellenistic Roman culture led to the theological adventures that produced the classical doctrines of Trinity and Incarnation, using the intellectual materials derived from middle-period Platonism. We now need an ecumenical theology of evil. At present we are too easily left stranded between personal guilt and atonement on the one hand and structural evil in society on the other. And when it is asserted that the gospel is addressed to both, we begin to quarrel about priorities. No one has done more than Andrew Kirk to point out the contradictions in this matter. Perhaps we need to consider more deeply what Paul calls the principalities and powers in charge of the course of the world, yet defeated by the Resurrection of Christ and dragged behind the triumphal chariot of the cross. And perhaps Christian worldviews with open frontiers between the phenomenal and transcendent world will give new vision to jaded theological activity. Perhaps a richer theology of the family, one that has place for the ancestors, will come as a richer family reality of

Africa and Asia than the atomized one of modernity. We need to reflect more on the implications of the Lord's words about Abraham, Isaac, and Jacob: "He is not the God of the dead, but of the living." This could be the most productive era for theology since the early centuries.

CHAPTER 6

Monks and Evangelicals

At any given time and place, the Christian nature of Christendom was at best a compromise, at worst a mockery. Society manifestly flouted the norms that Christendom proclaimed. But in many a time and place, there were people, men and women, who sought a truer, a more radical discipleship than Christendom usually revealed, and more than its normal structures sometimes permitted.

Such people often had the sense of sin in a very high degree; often they had gone through experiences of spiritual crisis. They tapped into an older Christian tradition that had begun in the Nile Valley in the middle years of the third century, when Antony the Copt sought the way to become the disciple whom Jesus spoke of in the Gospels, taking seriously the counsel to sell all and give to the poor, to take no thought for the morrow, to care only for the kingdom and its righteousness.

The monastic movement sought to reestablish the life of the apostolic church and to create a new community in which a consistent Christian life was possible. The communities were not separate from Christendom; they were integral to it. They had meaning only in relation to the wider Christian community. If the model of Christendom itself was Israel, and the model of the Christian prince was Hezekiah or Josiah, the model of the monastery was that of the Righteous Remnant, the true Israel that becomes an earnest of the wider Israel's salvation.

The monasteries, as with all human institutions, suffered from tendencies to corruption, and in Protestant lands were abandoned, for the Protestant Reformers sought the reformation of the whole church, not just a remnant. But in Protestant lands, the same features that had marked pre-Reformation Christendom were soon manifest; Protestant Christendom, like Catholic, veered between compromise and revival. And as in Catholic Christendom, so in Protestant Christendom, men and women sought a truer and more radical discipleship than a nominally Christian society offered or sometimes permitted.

Typically, a deep sense of guilt marked the beginning of this quest; typically, an immense, sometimes ecstatic sense of joy and deliverance followed, with the recognition that Christ's atonement brought forgiveness. And this experience of Christ's mercy was typically the entrance to a life of devout striving after the models of life depicted in the New Testament.

The monasteries were gone now, and the patterns of experience became more individualized; indeed, wider currents of thought that were stressing the autonomous nature of the self over against the older corporate sense of Christendom perhaps increased this tendency. Those who went this way typically sought others of like mind and like spirit and formed communities more or less formal.

The earliest models of this are to be found in the Anabaptist congregations of the Reformation period. Later versions appeared: the Puritan, particularly in the Anglo-Saxon lands; the Pietists, particularly in Germany and Central Europe; the evangelical, begun in the Anglo-Saxon world and merging into European Pietism. These movements are spiritual descendants of the earlier discipleship movements that brought people to the monastic orders and the societies. The Puritan, Pietist, and evangelical conversion movements can be seen as the heirs of these earlier medieval and early modern reformist strands within Christendom.

They are equally manifestations of Christian radicalism, and they are crucial to the nature and the history of the missionary movement; at crucial moments, they are the main sources of missionaries. Radical Christians are, generally speaking, converted people, and radical Christians, again generally speaking, are the stuff of which missionaries were made. Such people could not be satisfied with the compromises effected by nominally Christian governments, or with less than the widest proclamation of the gospel about Christ that they believed to be the vehicle of human salvation.

The new position of the powers of Christendom in the non-Western world seemed to lay an added burden, a new responsibility, to proclaim that message. It was necessary to have a new type of Christian proclamation, embodied in people who must offer and demonstrate but could not compel: preachers of the word who would be in a different position from any preacher in Christendom; preachers who must find a way of getting a hearing but could not command, who must learn a language and find a place within a strange society; people who would live on terms dictated by someone else. The fundamental missionary qualification is probably still the readiness to live on terms set by someone else.

The Enlightenment might have strangled Christianity in Europe, but in fact Christianity adapted to it and survived. In the process, the Puritan, Pietist, and evangelical movements played a vital part. They brought religion into the sphere of personal consciousness and personal decision and thus met the Cartesian threat, while generally retaining the concept of Christendom: recognition by the state and by society at large of Christian norms.

The radical movements, all in their different ways, distinguished between nominal, or formal, Christianity and real, or inward, Christianity. Pietist and evangelical religion are protests against a Christendom that is not Christian enough. And evangelical conversion is thus genetically related to that earlier protest against the inadequacies of Christendom, monastic conversion. Both produce forms of Christianity; both produce missionaries.

CHAPTER 7

When World Christianity Fell Apart

It is almost sixty years ago that I took my first faltering steps in academic research on the early church. I had the blessing of the guidance of one of the great patristic scholars of the day who floored me with his statement that we knew next to nothing about the church in the period before the Council of Nicaea in AD 325. Research on the early church was thus to be directed to remedying this situation, and I found myself gently but firmly led toward one of the hot topics of the day, the issue of whether there was a body of material, conveyed originally in oral form, from apostolic times still recoverable from later writings.

There was a third-century writing from Rome that made such claims. The trouble was that the Greek text of its original version had been lost, and we had it now only in translations—or were they adaptations? There was a very fragmentary Latin version, versions in two dialects of Coptic, in Arabic, and in Ethiopic. In addition, the work had clearly been quarried by two different Syriac works.

Here could I but have recognized it, I was being confronted by one of the most significant aspects of that ante-Nicaean church: its immense geographical spread and its linguistic and cultural diversity. But I missed it.

Following the lines of the day, the problem seemed to me to be the restoration of the original Greek text. And for that purpose the Latin version, fragmentary as it was, seemed to be the best guide; the Sahidic, the Bohairic, the Ethiopic, the Arabic, of much less use, and the Syriac works decidedly inferior. I did not solve the problem of the Apostolic Tradition. Nor did I add significantly to our understanding of the ante-Nicaean church. My one possible contribution was to raise new issues about the Latin text, which I suggested was in fact of Gothic origin. Gothic? A text originating in Rome, evidently treasured in Upper Egypt, in Lower Egypt, in Ethiopia, across a whole swath of the Middle East, that had also been drawn on by Goths.

I still did not get the point. The whole bias of my training, the whole outlook of contemporary patristic scholarship directed attention to the events and processes within the Roman Empire and to the Greek and Latin languages as the main keys to unlock them. Yet this callow young would-be scholar was handling a text that was evidently being read, pondered, altered, adapted in the Roman Empire, in the Persian Empire, deep in the Nile Valley, down into Ethiopia, out into that intensely mobile, completely open-ended Syriac-speaking world. Was that not potentially far more revealing about the early church and far more exciting than establishing the exact text of its rather cantankerous Roman author?

I can only plead my youth and inexperience, but most of my elders and betters were also in thrall to the same assumption: the primacy of the Roman Empire for understanding the context of the early church. And generation after generation perpetuated the habit by teaching early church history on the basis of events that took place in that part of the early church that lay within the Roman Empire and used Latin and Greek, passing over the massive area of Asia and Africa in which the church of the early centuries was present and active and among the languages in which the accounts of its actions, thinking, and worship are recorded.

As the missionary activity of the last couple of centuries offered theological education to the more recent churches of Africa and Asia and as those churches took over the books and the maps and the knowledge of their teachers, the old Christianity of Asia and Africa dropped out of sight. Everything seemed to reinforce the impression that the Christian faith was a late arrival in Asia and Africa and that it was an import from the West where it had been indigenous, its history inextricably entangled with and determined by events in European history involving popes and emperors and reformers and revivalists.

We have come in recent times to acknowledge that Christianity is global, a six-continent phenomenon, and that its center of gravity has now moved southward, with Africa especially, Asia, Latin America, and the Pacific together providing the majority of the world's Christians, and that proportion increasing year by year. There are welcome signs that this is becoming in itself a field of study and research. But the impression still remains that it is a recent phenomenon, a development of the twentieth century. In one sense this is incontrovertible. The early church knew nothing of the Americas or the Pacific, and its presence in Africa was partial and in Southeast Asia nugatory. Nevertheless, the first six or seven centuries of the church saw an expansion of the Christian faith across vast areas of the landmass that constitutes Europe, Asia, and Africa, a Christian faith expressed in a multitude of cultures and civilizations, and using a multitude of languages.

Christianity in fact from its beginning has been, in principle, global, and for long centuries was so in practice. The contemporary fact of global Christianity is not a new development, but a return to normality, a return to the multicentric, multilingual, multicultural reality of the early church that preceded those exceptional centuries when Christianity was an overwhelmingly Western religion with its cultural and linguistic expression determined by the peoples of Europe and their descendants elsewhere. The governing vision of the church of Christ, after all, is of a great multitude that no one can count from every nation, ethnicity, people, and language.

Multiculturalism is implicit in the New Testament model of the church. When the movement that came to be called Christianity began in the Roman province of Judea, its membership was wholly Jewish. Its first great center of growth was Jerusalem, and to judge from the New Testament evidence, the movement made considerable inroads into segments of Jerusalem society of different cultural and linguistic orientation, Hebraist and Hellenist.

When as in the affair of provision for widows in Acts 6, the cracks along cultural lines appeared, the apostolic leadership quickly took steps to defuse the situation. It is somewhat anachronistic to call the Jerusalem church "Christian." Its members saw themselves as Israel of the Messianic Age. They had no idea of having changed their religion by the outcome of their faith in Jesus. That religion was a converted form of what they had before, a converted Judaism, Jewish life lived in the light of the messiahship of Jesus, an actualization of the prophetic view as a people bearing the law of God written on their hearts.

The movement vigorously proclaimed the messiahship of Jesus to the indigenous Jewish community and, when partially ejected from Jerusalem, to diaspora Jews also. But despite the words recorded as the Great Commission, they were much less ready to approach those who were not ethnic Jews. The New Testament records a series of incidents—Peter and Cornelius,

Philip and the Samarians, the Ethiopian eunuch—that forced this issue on the church's thinking.

The first major breakthrough seems to have occurred in Antioch when a group of refugees from Jerusalem spoke about Jesus to Greek-speaking pagans, using the title "Lord," which had resonances both in Jewish tradition and in Hellenistic pagan religion, in preference to the "messiah" concept as the focus of presentation.

The result was a bicultural Jesus-worshiping community in Antioch that now needed a name of its own and adopted or was accorded the title "Christian." The word "Christian," therefore, exists only because of the bicultural nature of the community that it first described. To be Christian is implicitly to belong to a community that is not monocultural. Antioch developed as a mission center, producing other ethnically mixed churches across Anatolia.

The essentially bicultural nature of the church was recognized by an overwhelmingly observant Jewish church leadership at the so-called Apostolic Council described in Acts 15. There had been a significant movement to treat Gentile followers of Jesus as proselytes, requiring them to receive circumcision and keep the Torah. Once the principle was established that neither circumcision nor Torah was a requirement for Gentile Christians—Paul indeed goes further, insisting that it is not even an option for Gentile Christians—the principle of biculturalism was formally enshrined, for Jewish believers continued to be subject to both Law and circumcision, and Paul accepts that this is rightly so.

Yet just as the Jerusalem church embodied a form of converted Judaism, so Acts 15 implicitly required that the religion of Gentile Christians be a converted form of Hellenistic culture. We see that Hellenistic way of being Christian in the process of construction in the Epistles of Paul, and the Epistle to the Ephesians shows how two segments of social reality, converted Judaism and converted Hellenistic culture, are equally necessary as building blocks in the new temple that was being built in which Jew and Gentile would worship together. Converted Judaism and converted Christ-directed Hellenistic society were necessary to each other in the economy of God.

Jerusalem remained the respected mother church of all as the Gentile mission continued and as the Hellenistic Gentile element in it increasingly dominated, and when famine and distress struck it, the overwhelmingly Gentile churches displayed solidarity with it by generous donations. But the Jewish War of 66 to 70 all but destroyed its social base. An increasing Jewish hostility to the Christian Way and the sheer success of the Gentile mission in the Hellenistic world caused the original bicultural model of the church to give way to a Christian lifestyle representing a converted form of Greco-Roman culture, drawing heavily on its vocabulary and thought processes.

The eclipse of the original bicultural model of the church, however, proved to be the prelude to the development of a new multicultural model, for from this period the spread of the Christian faith moves in three general directions: westward across the Roman Empire, including the lands on all the shores of the Mediterranean; eastward with the Arab peoples at the fore, into the Persian Empire and beyond it, across the Asian landmass; and southward by way of the Nile Valley and the Horn of Africa and by way of south Arabia to south India.

Over a period of some six centuries, a remarkable expansion of the Christian faith took place in all three directions. The Roman Empire produced the major example, though there were several significant examples in Asia, too, of the acceptance of the faith by the authorities of the state. Such political acceptance, however, followed a long period in which Christianity gradually made headway in different locations within the Roman Empire and in different branches of society, the old Roman aristocracy being the last to yield.

The diffusion took place through many sources. One used the apparatus of the indigenous institution of the philosophical school. The resultant prolonged interaction between Christianity and the Greek philosophical tradition had a surprising outcome. At one time Christianity and Greek intellectual culture had been held to be incompatible. But not only did Christian thinking and writing weather the Greek intellectual attack; Greek philosophy, as later Roman legal theory, was put into Christian service with lasting results for Christian theology and the emergence of the creeds and other formularies.

At first the Roman state saw Christianity as potentially disruptive, an assessment given support by the Christian refusal to participate in ritual acts of civil religion involving sacrifice to the imperial genius. The state instituted persecution, at first sporadic and local, designed to control undue expansion, later centralized and systematic, aimed at destroying Christian leadership and organization, and finally, in the reign of Diocletian, all-out attack on Christians. Despite large numbers of Christians lapsing under persecution, the popular movement toward Christianity continued with wide recognition of its beneficial moral and social effects.

With the accession to power of Constantine, the era of persecution ended and one of steadily increasing imperial favor opened. There is no single date for the fall of Roman paganism. Local communities took into their own hands the issue of overthrowing the altars when they felt strong enough to do so. Greek-speaking East and Latin-speaking West united in Christian profession. Egypt, Syria, Asia Minor, North Africa became leading centers of Christian life and thought. The spread of Christianity within the empire was not always matched by evangelistic activity beyond it.

There were notable successes. The Goth Wulfila (Ulfilas), who died about 381, descended from Christian prisoners from Pontus seized by Gothic raiders at an earlier time, brought a major movement of the Goths toward the Christian faith, and brought about the translation of the Scriptures into the Gothic language. Patrick, who died around 461, a Celtic captive from Romanized Britain taken prisoner to Ireland, became a notable missionary there.

On the other hand, impact on the North African desert and mountain peoples seems to have been minimal. The political reality was that Rome, whether under Christian or pre-Christian rule, had difficulty maintaining its extended frontiers against the peoples to the north and south, and also against the superpower Persia to the east. The converted Goths moved from their homeland into Roman territory. The great age of barbarian conversion accompanied and followed the collapse of the western half of the Roman Empire.

The Acts of the Apostles reflects an early stage of the westward movement that we have described. But there is one point at which Luke takes the account in another direction. This is in chapter 8 with the story of the Ethiopian eunuch, who is last seen by his evangelist as rejoicing on his way back into the heart of Africa as a baptized believer in Jesus the Messiah. With this story Luke points to the fact that there are other stories of the spread of the gospel beyond the one that is his main narrative; in particular, there is a southward expansion into the heart of Africa. A significant part of this story concerns Egypt; pre-Arab Egypt, let us remember, with centuries of presence there of the dark-skinned Kushite peoples; and the Nile Valley in particular. Egypt at the time lay within the Roman Empire, and Alexandria, its bustling metropolis, and other major towns were part of the Greek world.

But the rural areas reflected a different cultural milieu, and Coptic, the vernacular speech derived from ancient Egyptian, stubbornly held on. In this Coptic-speaking rural area, Christianity seems to have spread early and widely. The version in the Sahidic dialect of Coptic is one of the earliest Bible translations of all. The story of Antony who was born in or about 251 shows us a typical African villager and the archetype of African Christianity. Antony represents an early movement of religious revival. The movement is radical, biblicist, spiritually confrontational, marked by a deep sense of the reality of the spirit world, of the activity of evil powers, the necessity for spiritual combat, and the completeness of Christ's victory in such combat. Coptic Christianity produced a core of devoted radical Christians, and in the monastic movement, it developed a way of organizing them as a disciplined force.

A church began to develop in Axum, a state in the Horn of Africa, in the early fourth century, and the inscriptions of the Axumite king Ezana suggest that this national movement occurred during his reign, from polytheism to monotheism and then to open Christian allegiance. Rufinus associates this change with the work of two Christians shipwrecked on the Eritrean coast and pressed into the Axumite royal service. He also shows how an early link was forged between this church and that in Egypt. Up the Nile, south of Egypt in what we think of as the Sudan Republic, lay African states collectively called Nubia by the Romans.

Greek historians relate how in 543 the emperor Justinian and his wife Theodora sent embassies to the three Nubian states that issued in their conversion. Archaeology has revealed the dimension missing from this story, the fact that Christianity had already been present in Nubia for at least 150 years. The embassies thus mark, not the first coming of the gospel to the Nubian states, but acceptance by their rulers of what had already been adopted by many of their people. The states eventually combined in a single Christian kingdom. The Christian history requires the fuller interpretation of the archaeological data, but that kingdom lasted a thousand years.

Thus, by AD 600 there was a significant and still expanding Christian presence in eastern Africa, centered on the Nile Valley and the Ethiopian Plateau. Meanwhile the Christian message was increasingly embraced among Syriac-speaking peoples of the empire's eastern frontier, on both sides of it. It is impossible to chart its early spread beyond those borders; no doubt there were initiatives, probably beginning, as in the Roman Empire, with Jewish communities in different centers. Certainly Edessa, a small principality serving as a buffer between the Roman and Persian Empires and eventually incorporated in the Roman, was a particularly important Christian center. Christianity spread through Mesopotamia until the majority of the population of what is now Iraq probably professed the Christian faith, producing a vigorous church that in the succeeding centuries provided the intellectual centers for Eastern Christianity and produced a core of missionaries.

A poem written in the early third century celebrates Christian communities in the provinces of Iran and among the desert Arabs, whose social and cultural practices it claims had been transformed as a result. The Christian impact on Iran was increased by further mass deportations of Syrian Christians later in the third century to work on the massive building projects. By the fourth century Merv, in what is now the borderland of Iran and Afghanistan, was accounted a Christian territory.

Though so strong in Mesopotamia, Christianity never had the runaway effect on the Iranian Empire that it did on the Roman, and there was never a Persian Constantine. There were many martyrs, notably during the fourth century, in response to an appeal by Constantine on behalf of Iranian Christians. Yet it is clear that Christianity penetrated priestly and royal circles, and when the last Zoroastrian emperor died, fleeing from the Arab Muslims, it was Christian monks who buried him. Christian interaction with Iranian culture produced a major new religion in Manichaeism.

By the end of the fifth century, Christianity was expanding well beyond the Persian Empire. In 549 the Bactrian Huns declared themselves a Christian people. Their church had been founded by Arab Christians sold to them as slaves. In the same period the Himyar kingdom of ancient Yemen became Christian.

Christian expansion in Asia took place by three principal means. The discipline of the Syriac Church was designed to produce spiritual athletes who were in a real sense temples of the Holy Spirit, and these included missionaries ready for extreme conditions. But Christian families traveled widely to trade and settled far from home and formed congregations and called ministers, and refugees from persecution or from harassment formed other important bridgeheads, notably in India. The trade routes by land and sea drew both the settled families and the missionaries. The sea route to India, fed by the monsoon, may have drawn one of the earliest missionaries of all.

Persistent and multiform tradition, Hindu as well as Christian, associates the apostle Thomas with India, as do the old Christian communities there, and identifies the site at Mylapore, near Chennai, with his death. The early-third-century Acts of Judas Thomas is a novel, not a history work, but it was written by someone with real knowledge of India, and the possibility of Jewish communities may well have drawn the apostle there. What is certain is that from early centuries there was a significant worshiping Christian community in India that met the first Christians from the West in the sixteenth century and remains there to this day.

Syriac sources refer to churches in Sri Lanka and raise the issue whether there were any beyond, presumably pointing the way with the trade winds to Southeast Asia. The landward route was the Silk Road to China across Central Asia. Here there is abundant evidence of the traders and the missionaries. In the sixth century a Turkic king was converted, and thereafter the Christian presence developed among the various Turkic peoples surrounding the Chinese Empire. Samarkand on the Silk Road became a center of church activity. To the north the nomadic peoples had an organized church, their bishop traveling with them, his cathedral a tent.

As noted earlier, in 635 Christian mission reached the court of the emperor of China, was politely received, perhaps because China, a rising power, was now taking an interest in the affairs, including the religious affairs, of its neighbors. The emperor's desire to study the Scriptures and their teaching took Christians into a new world of thought and expression with new challenges for translation. The process of translation and study took three years, after which the emperor announced his approval of Christian teaching and permission for its propagation. The terms of the edict announcing this suggest that the teaching appeared to the emperor to be in accord with Confucian moral and social values.

An inscription erected in 781 gives an account of the first 150 years of Chinese Christianity, with periods of favor and periods of disfavor. Its later history is problematical, and the ultimate fate of the Luminous religion, as it was called, brought first by

Arab missionaries in the seventh century, remains mysterious. Changing conditions making new discoveries possible may provide more light on this. But there is tantalizing evidence for interaction between Christian and Buddhist missionaries. The twentieth-century Norwegian scholar-missionary Karl Ludvig Reichelt argued that this contact with early Christianity moved Chinese Buddhism into new directions, opening it to the need for a savior and producing a doctrine of grace.

A recurrent feature of Christian history in China has been the problem of religious vocabulary and how both Confucian and Buddhist sources can be drawn on for the purpose. This missiological crux was then that, by the seventh century, Christianity was in principle global and, indeed, had become so in practice. It had spread over a considerable part of the then known world and was still expanding. It straddled the Eurasian landmass from the Atlantic almost to the Pacific.

When the emperor of China was first looking at the Christian message in the Scriptures, the king of Northumbria was hearing the proclamation of the gospel for the first time in northern England. There were important exceptions. The Roman Empire, with its fear of the barbarians and the possibility of the collapse of the frontiers, perhaps inhibited much mission activity beyond those frontiers. The tenuousness of the Christian presence among the desert peoples of North Africa has already been mentioned, precluding any further spread to sub-Saharan Africa. And though Arab Christianity was so strong in the most populated Arab locations, it had little hold on the tribes of the interior of Arabia. Syriac was the primary language of Arab Christianity to the north, Latin of North Africa. Significantly, there is no pre-Islamic translation of the Scriptures into either Arabic or Berber.

But Christian expansion has never been a matter of uninterrupted steady progress or unresisted advance, and between the fifth and seventh centuries, a series of developments helped to turn back the tide of advance and inflict serious loss on the Christian church.

The first was the collapse of the Western Roman Empire. There is no single datable event, of course, for this; it was a process. Augustine died in 430. Its early manifestations: the barbarian sacking of Rome and the Vandal invasion of North Africa. Thereafter, despite periods of recovery, the story is of falling frontiers, invading peoples from the north, establishment of barbarian kingdoms, usually initially pagan, in what had been Roman and Christian areas. In some of those areas, notably North Africa, the church declined or ceased to matter. In others, endemic warfare brought weakness. Constantine, realizing that the empire's center of gravity lay in the East now, had moved his capital to the new Rome on the Bosphorus, Constantinople. Thus, the Christian Roman Empire, now Greek-speaking, continued for some time to come. The Greek Church had no Middle Ages; the patristic period extended there to the fifteenth century. But inevitably events in the Western Empire meant that Western and Eastern Christians would in future follow different paths.

We saw that the New Testament model of the church was bicultural. By the second century that model had almost disappeared. It had been succeeded by a multicultural and multicentric church, for despite the doctrinal division, especially in the Greek world, and in particular the Arian controversy that disrupted the church, Christians west, east, and south continued to recognize one another as belonging to a single great church. The Greek word *oikoumene*, the whole world, could also be used within the Roman Empire, as it is indeed in the beginning of Luke's Gospel, for the whole Roman world. In the days of the Christian empire it was easy to think of the church less as a worldwide than as an empire-wide institution.

Just as pagan emperors had persecuted Christians in the interest of imperial unity, Christian emperors found that religious disharmony was potentially destructive of the empire. Constantine began the process when in 325 he sought to end the Arian controversy through a council of the whole church called at Nicaea. But he at least recognized that the church is a worldwide, not just an empire-wide, institution. And a small number of bishops from beyond the empire did attend Nicaea. Later emperors saw no such necessity.

The Council of Chalcedon, for instance, called in 451 to settle matters of Christology for the peace of the Roman Empire, had no one from beyond its frontiers. In effect, Chalcedon produced a framework that satisfied most of those who did their theological thinking in Latin and those who did their theological thinking in Greek. It did not satisfy those who thought in Coptic or Syriac. Large numbers of Syriac and Coptic Christians were alienated as a result. The situation became far worse in the following century as successive imperial governments tried to impose the Chalcedonian formula by force. The bitter fruit was seen at the time of the Muslim conquest.

In effect, the sixth century saw the breakup of the great multicultural church and its division along linguistic and cultural lines. The ecumenical tragedy that it produced has been hidden by concentration on the Greek or Latin doctrinal debate on Christology. Names such as Nestorian and Monophysite have been applied as anathemas. The majority of Syriac-speaking Christians and the majority of Coptic speakers in Egypt and almost all other African Christians in Ethiopia and Nubia followed these confessions.

The division has been permanent, and there were two long-term effects. One was that the Christians of Europe became cut off from the Christians of Asia and Africa. Second, further divisions of the church along linguistic and cultural lines became easier until they became taken for granted. The New Testament norm of the multicultural church passed from view. That eclipse marked the breakup of the original global Christianity.

Events that followed brought the rise of Islam and with it the Arab Empire in which both Monophysite Christians in Egypt and the Nestorian and Monophysite Christians in Syria found the Arabs to be the liberators from Christian oppressors. The emergence of the Mongols and their eventual, though not inevitable, decision for Islam heralded the eclipse of early Asian Christianity. And events in the Christian world ensured that its remnants and the beleaguered remnants of early African Christianity were cut off from Christians in Europe.

The dominant form of Christianity became one acculturated over centuries to European thought, language, and conditions. And Europeans came to assume that theirs was, if not the only form of Christianity, at least the only authentic form. The legacy of the collapse in the sixth century of the first expression of global Christianity has been burdensome.

But we are now in a new age of world Christianity, even larger, even more diverse than the earlier model, but like it multicentric, multilingual, multicultural. And it operates under conditions that permit a new start. Perhaps the acid test for Christianity in the twenty-first century will be whether the sixth-century legacy can be repaired and whether African and Indian and Chinese and Japanese and Korean and North and

South American and East and West European Christianity can each present a convincing segment of converted social reality, each forming a building block in the new temple, sharing and cohering together in the body of Christ.

Epilogue

CHAPTER 8

Conversion and Christian Continuity

From Pentecost to the twentieth century, Christian history may be divided into six phases. Each phase sees its embodiment in a major culture area, which means that in that phase Christianity took an impress from the culture of that area. In each phase the expression of the Christian faith developed features that could only have originated in that culture and within that phase.

For one brief, vital period, Christianity was entirely Jewish. First-generation Christians were all Jews—diverse, perhaps, in background and outlook, Hebraist and Hellenist, conservative and liberal—but without the slightest idea that they had "changed their religion" by recognizing Jesus as Messiah. It remains one of the marvels of the ages that Christianity entered its second phase at all. But those unnamed "men of Cyprus and Cyrene" introduced some Greek-speaking pagans in Antioch to the Jewish national savior (Acts 11:20), and those law-righteous apostles and elders at Jerusalem agreed that they might enter Israel without becoming Jews (Acts 15:1–29). The result was that Christianity became Hellenistic-Roman; the Messiah, Savior of Israel, was recognized to be also the Lord, Savior of souls. It happened just in time, for soon afterward the Jewish state disappeared in the early holocausts of AD 70 and AD 135. Only the timely diffusion of faith in Jesus across cultural lines gave that faith any continuing place in the world. Without its diffusion at that time, its principal representatives would have been the Ebionites and similar groups who by the third and fourth centuries lay on the very fringe of the Christian movement, even if they could claim to be the enduring legacy of James the Just and the Jerusalem elders.

In the process of transmission, the expression of that faith changed beyond what many an outsider might recognize. To see the extent of the change one has only to look at the utterances of early Jewish Christians as reflected in the New Testament, utterances that indicate their priorities, the matters most on their hearts. "We had hoped that he would be the one . . . to set Israel free," says the disillusioned disciple on the way to Emmaus (Lk 24:21, TEV). On the Mount of Ascension, the preoccupation is the same. Realizing that they stand at the threshold of a new era, the disciples ask, "Lord, will you at this time give the kingdom back to Israel?" (Acts 1:6). Statements and questions like these could be uttered only by Jews, out of centuries of present suffering and hope deferred. They have no meaning for those who belong to the nations, whether in the first or the twentieth century. Each comes to Jesus with quite different priorities, and those priorities shape the questions they ask, even about salvation. A first-century Levantine Gentile would never have brought to Jesus as a matter of urgency the question of the political destiny of Israel, though he might have asked about the destiny of the soul.

Those Christian Jews in Antioch who realized that Jesus had something to say to their pagan friends took an immense risk. They were prepared to drop the time-honored word "Messiah," knowing that it would mean little to their neighbors and perhaps mislead them—what concern was the redeemer of Israel, should they grasp the concept, to them? They were prepared to see the title of their national savior, the fulfillment of the dearest hopes of their people, become attached to the name of Jesus as though it was a sort of surname. They took up the ambiguous and easily misunderstood word "Lord" (Acts 11:20; cf. Acts 9:22, which relates to a Jewish audience). They could not have foreseen where their action would lead, and it would be surprising if someone did not warn them about the disturbing possibilities of confusion and syncretism. But it transformed Christianity.

The Second Age of Christianity

The second of the six phases of Christianity was Hellenistic-Roman. This is not to say that within that age Christianity was geographically confined to the area where Hellenistic-Roman culture was dominant. Important Christian communities lay, for instance, in Central Asia, East Africa, and South India. But the dominant expression of the Christian faith for several centuries resulted from its steady penetration of Hellenistic thought and culture during a period when that culture was also associated with a single political entity, the Roman Empire.

The second phase has, like the first, left its mark on all later Christianity. Of the new religious ideas that entered with the Christian penetration of Hellenistic culture, one of the most permeative for the future was that of orthodoxy, a canon of right belief, capable of being stated in a series of propositions arrived at by a process of logical argument. Such a feature was not likely to mark Christianity in its Jewish period; Jewish identity has always been concerned either with what a person *is* or with what he *does* rather than with what he *believes*. But when Christian faith began to penetrate the Hellenistic-Roman world, it encountered a total system of thought, a system to which it was in some respects antipathetic, but which, once encountered, had to be permeated. The system had a certain built-in arrogance, a feature it has never quite lost despite the mutations through which the Hellenistic-Roman legacy has gone in its transmission over the centuries to other peoples, and despite the penetration effected by Christian faith. Basically it maintained that there is one desirable pattern of life, a single "civilization" in effect, one model of society, one body of law, one universe of ideas. Accordingly, there are in essence two types of humanity: people who share that pattern and those ideas, and people who do not. There are Greeks—a cultural, not an ethnic, term—and there are barbarians. There are civilized people who share a common heritage, and there are savages, who do not.

In many ways the Jews and their religion already represented a challenge to this assumption. Whatever degree of assimilation to it many Jews might reflect, the stubborn fact of Jewish identity put them in a different category from the rest of the Hellenistic-Roman universe. Alone in that universe they had an alternative literature, a written tradition, of comparable antiquity. And they had their own dual classification of mankind: Israel— *the* nation—and the nations. Hellenistic-Roman Christians had no option but to maintain, and to seek to reconcile, aspects of both their inheritances.

The total Hellenistic-Roman system of thought had to be penetrated and Christianized by the gospel. This meant the endeavor to bring the intellectual tradition into captivity to Christ and to use it for new purposes; it also meant putting the traditions of codification and of organization to the service of the gospel. The result was orthodoxy, a logically expounded belief set in codified form, established through a process of consultation and maintained through effective organization. Hellenistic-Roman civilization offered a total system of thought and expected general conformity to its norms.

The Christian penetration of the system inevitably left it a total system.

The Third Age: Barbarian Christianity

Hellenistic-Roman civilization lived for centuries in the shadow of fear—fear of the day when the center could not hold, when things fell apart, when the overextended frontiers collapsed and the barbarian hordes poured in. Christians fully shared these fears. Tertullian, who lived in the age of persecution, though he would not countenance Christians in the army—Christ has unbelted every soldier, he says—prayed for the preservation of the empire; for when the frontiers collapsed, the great tribulation would begin. For people living under the Christian empire, the triumph of the barbarians would be equated with the end of Christian civilization.

Two great events brought about the end of Hellenistic-Roman Christianity. One had been widely predicted—the collapse of the Western Roman Empire before the barbarians. The other no one could have predicted—the emergence of the Arabs as a world power and their occupation of the Eastern provinces where the oldest and strongest Christian churches lay. The combination of these forces led to the end of the Hellenistic-Roman phase of Christianity. That it did not lead to the slow strangulation of the total Christian presence in the world was due to the slow, painful, and far from satisfactory spread of Christian allegiance among the tribal peoples beyond the old frontiers, the people known as barbarians, the destroyers of Christian civilization. What, in fact, happened was the development of a third phase of Christianity, what we may call a barbarian phase. Once again, it was just in time: centuries of erosion and attrition faced the peoples of Christianity's Hellenistic heartlands. Once again, Christianity had been saved by its cross-cultural diffusion.

The culture gap to be bridged was quite as great as that between Jew and Greek, yet the former faith of classical civilization became the religion of peasant cultivators. The process was marked by the more or less ready acceptance by new Christians of a great deal of the cultural inheritance belonging to the classical civilization from which they derived their Christianity. Further, when they substituted the God of the Bible for their traditional pantheons, the language and ideas had passed through a Greek-Roman filter before it reached them. The significance of this we must consider later.

Nevertheless, the barbarian phase was emphatically not a simple extension of the Christianity of the patristic age; it was a new creation, conditioned less by city-based literary, intellectual, and technological tradition than by the circumstances of peasant cultivators and their harsh, uncertain lives. If the barbarians took their ideas from the Hellenistic Christian world, they took their attitudes from the primal world; and both ideas and attitudes are components in the complex that makes up a people's religion. As with their predecessors, they appropriated the Christian faith for themselves, and reformulated it with effects that continued amid their successors after their own phase had passed away. If the second phase of Christianity invented the idea of orthodoxy, the third invented the idea of the Christian nation. Christian Roman emperors might establish the church, might punish heretics, might make laws claiming allegiance to Christ, might claim to represent Christ, but tribal peoples knew a far stronger law than any emperor could enforce—that of custom. Custom is binding upon every child born into a primal community; nonconformity to that custom is simply unthinkable. A communal decision to adopt the Christian faith might take some time in coming; there might be uncertainty, division, and debate, but once thoroughly made, the decision would bind everyone in that society. A community must have a single custom. It was not necessarily a case of strong rulers enforcing their own choice. In Iceland, which was a democracy with no central ruler, the assembly was divided down the middle between Christians and non-Christians. When the decision for Christianity was eventually made, the non-Christians felt bitter and betrayed, but no one suggested a division into communities with different religions. Religion, in fact, is but one aspect of the custom that binds a society together. There can be only one church in a community. And so barbarian Christianity brings to fruition the idea of the Christian nation.

Once the idea of the Christian nation was established, a new hermeneutic habit easily developed; the parallel between the Christian nation and Israel. Once nation and church are coterminous in scope, the experiences of the nation can be interpreted in terms of the history of Israel. In Western Christianity, this habit has long outlived the historical circumstances that gave it birth and has continued into the age of pluralism and secularization.

The Fourth and Fifth Ages of Christianity

The fourth cultural phase of Christianity was a natural development of the third. Interaction between Christian faith and practice in its Hellenistic-Roman form and the culture of the northern peoples produced a remarkably coherent system across Western and Central

Europe. When the Eastern Roman Empire, which effectively prolonged the Hellenistic phase of Christianity for several centuries in one area of the world, finally collapsed before the Muslims, this new hybrid Western form of Christianity became the dominant representation of Christianity. In the sixteenth century this Western formulation was to undergo radical revision through the movements of the Reformation. The Protestant version of this was particularly radical, not least—through its emphasis on vernacular Scriptures—in stressing the local encounter of man with the Word of God. Reforming Catholicism, on the other hand, stressed the universal nature of the church, but unconsciously established its universality on the basis of features that belonged essentially to Western intellectual and social history—and largely to a particular period of it. Both forms, however, belonged unmistakably to Western Europe; their very differences marked a growing cultural divergence between the north and south of the area.

One major development that took place within the West over those centuries set a challenge to Christian faith as hitherto received in Europe and required its reformulation. As we have seen, a necessary feature of barbarian Christianity was communal decision and mass response. But Western thought developed a particular consciousness of the individual as a monad, independent of kin-related identity. Christianity in its Western form adapted to this developing consciousness, until the concept of Christian faith as a matter of individual decision and individual application became one of the hallmarks of Western Christianity.

This Western phase of Christianity developed into another, with which it should probably be taken: the age of expanding Europe. The population of Europe was exported to other continents and the dominance of Europe extended until, by the twentieth century, people of European origin occupied, possessed, or dominated the greater part of the globe. During this vital period, Christianity was the professed and, to a considerable extent, the active religion of almost all the European peoples.

Seen in the context of Christian history as a whole, this period saw two remarkable developments. One was a substantial recession of European peoples from the Christian faith. Its significance was not at first manifest because it was not regular and steady. Beginning in the sixteenth century, it had reached notable proportions by the eighteenth, when it appeared as if Christianity might still claim the masses of Europe but was losing the intellectuals. In the eighteenth century, however, and for much of the nineteenth, there was a Christian counterattack, which halted the movement of recession in Europe and brought spectacular accessions in the new towns of North America. The sudden quickening of the recession, therefore, in the twentieth century took observers by surprise—though predictions of its extent had been generally accepted a couple of centuries earlier. Only in the twentieth century did it become clear that the great towns, which were the source and the sign of Europe's dominance, had never really been evangelized at all.

The other major development of the period was the cross-cultural transplantation of Christianity, with varying degrees of success, to multitudes of people outside Europe. It did not look overwhelming by 1920; the high hopes, once entertained, of the evangelization of the world in one generation had by that time drained away into the trenches of the First World War. But we can see now that it was enough. The seeds of Christian faith had been planted in the Southern continents; before long these seeds were bearing abundant fruit. All the world empires, except the Russian, have now passed away;

the European hegemony of the world is broken; the recession of Christianity among the European peoples appears to be continuing. And yet we seem to stand at the threshold of a new age of Christianity, one in which its main base will be in the Southern continents, and where its dominant expression will be filtered through the culture of those continents. Once again, Christianity has been saved for the world by its diffusion across cultural lines.

Christian Expansion and the Sixth Age of Christianity

Let us pause here to consider the peculiar history of Christianity, as compared with other faiths. Hindus say with some justice that they represent the world's earliest faith, for many things in Indian religion are the same now as they were before Israel came out of Egypt. Yet over all those centuries, the geographical and cultural center has been the same. Invaders like the Aryans have come and made their mark; great innovative movements like that of the Buddha have come, flourished awhile, and then passed on elsewhere. The Christians and the Muslims with their claims to universal allegiance have come and made their converts. But still the same faith remains in the same place, absorbing all sorts of influences from without, not being itself absorbed by any.

By contrast, Iranian religion has been vital enough to have a molding effect at certain crucial times on Hinduism, Judaism, Christianity, and Islam in succession; and yet, as a separate, identifiable phenomenon in the world, its presence today is tiny. Christianity, on the other hand, has throughout its history spread outward, across cultural frontiers, so that each new point on the Christian circumference is a new potential Christian center. And the very survival of Christianity as a separate faith has evidently been linked to the process of cross-cultural transmission. Indeed, with hindsight, we can see that on several occasions this transmission took place just in time; that without it, the Christian faith must surely have withered away. Nor has its progress been steadily outward, as Muslims may claim of their faith. Its progress has been serial, with a principal presence in different parts of the world at different times.

Each phase of Christian history has seen a transformation of Christianity as it has entered and penetrated another culture. There is no such thing as "Christian culture" or "Christian civilization" in the sense that there is an Islamic culture and an Islamic civilization. There have been several different Christian civilizations already; there may yet be many more. The reason for this lies in the infinite translatability of the Christian faith. Islam, the only other faith hitherto to make a comparable impact in such global terms, can produce a simple, recognizable culture—recognizable despite local assimilations and variations—across its huge geographical spread. This surely has something to do with the ultimate untranslatability of its charter document, the Koran. The Christian Scriptures, by contrast, are open to translation; nay, the great act on which Christian faith rests, the Word becoming flesh and pitching tent among us, is itself an act of translation. And this principle brings Christ to the heart of each culture, to the points of reference within it by which men know themselves. That is why each phase of Christian history has produced new themes— themes that the points of reference of that culture have made inescapable for those who share that framework. The same themes may lie beyond the conception of Christians of an earlier or another framework of thought. They will have their own commanding heights to be conquered by Christ.

Diversity and Coherence in Historic Christianity

If we were to take samples of *representative* Christians from every century from the first to the twentieth, moving from place to place as will be necessary if our choice is to be representative, would they have anything in common? Certainly such a collection of people would often have quite different priorities in the expression of the faith. And it is not only that the priorities are different; what appears of utmost importance to one group may appear intolerable, even blasphemous, to another. Even were we to take only those acknowledged as forming the tradition of Christianity represented by Western Evangelicals—how does the expression of faith compare among temple-worshiping Jew, Greek Council father, Celtic monk, German Reformer, English Puritan, Victorian churchman? How defective would each think the other on matters vital to religion?

And yet I believe we can discern a firm coherence underlying all these and, indeed, the whole of historic Christianity. It is not easy to state this coherence in propositional, still less in credal form—for extended credal formulation is itself a necessary product of a particular Christian culture. But a small body of convictions and responses express themselves when Christians of any culture express their faith. These may perhaps be stated thus:

1. *The worship of the God of Israel.* This not only defines the nature of God—the One, the Creator and the Judge, the One who does right and before whom man falls down— it makes the historical particularity of Christian faith. And it links the Christian—usually a Gentile—with the history of a people quite different from his own. It gives him a point of reference outside himself and his society.

2. *The ultimate significance of Jesus of Nazareth.* This is perhaps the test that above all marks off historic Christianity from the various movements along its fringes, as well as from other world faiths that accord recognition to the Christ. Once again, it would be pointless to try to encapsulate this ultimacy forever in any one credal formula. Any such formula will be superseded; or, even if adopted for traditional reasons, it may make no impression on believers who do not have the conceptual vocabulary the formula will imply. Each culture has its ultimate; and Christ is the ultimate in everyone's vocabulary.

3. *That God is active where believers are.*

4. *That believers constitute a people of God transcending time and space.*

These convictions appear to underlie the whole Christian tradition across the centuries, in all its diversity. Some of the very diversity of Christian expression has itself arisen from the need to set forth these responses in terms of the believers' framework of thought and perception of the world. To them we should perhaps add a small body of institutions that have continued from century to century. The most obvious of these have been the reading of a common body of Scriptures and the special use of bread and wine and water.

Southern Culture and the Christian Future

Once more the Christian faith is penetrating new cultures—those of Africa and the Pacific and parts of Asia. (The Latin American situation is too complex for us to consider its peculiar significance here.) The present indications are that these southern expressions of Christianity are becoming the dominant forms of the faith.

This is likely to mean the appearance of new themes and priorities undreamed of by ourselves or by earlier Christian ages; for it is the mark of Christian faith that it must bring Christ to the big issues closest to men's hearts. It does so through the structures by which people perceive and recognize their world; these are not universally the same. Affirmations that have been keynotes for Christians of former ages—or for ourselves—often represent the application of the Word about Christ to some great issue of assumption within the culture of time.

For Christians of another time and place, with different cultural issues and assumptions, the notes may sound faint or strange. But there will certainly be themes and assumptions within their cultures that await the Word about Christ; and as the word is applied, new Christian keynotes may be heard. Southern Christianity may not possess those points of reference that made orthodoxy, for instance, or the Christian nation, or the primacy of individual decision, absolutely crucial to the capture by Christ of older worldviews. Pious early Jewish Christians would have found their Greek successors strangely cold about Israel's most precious possession, the Law of God and its guide to living. Many of them would have been equally disturbed by the intellectual complexities into which Christological discussion was leading Greek Christians.

In each case what was happening was the working out of Christian faith within accepted views of the world, so that those worldviews—as with the conversion of believers—are transformed, yet recognizable. Conversion is not simply a personal matter; when applied to attitudes and priorities, relationships, and ways of thinking, it takes generations.

Sources

Prologue

Portions originally published as "Converts of Proselytes? The Crisis over the Conversion in the Early Church," *International Bulletin of Missionary Research* 28, no. 1 (January 2004): 2–6.

Chapters 1–4

"A Cultural History of the Christian Faith: Eusebius Revisited and Latourette Reconsidered." Fuller Theological Seminary Missiology Lectures, 1996.

Chapter 5

A revised version of chapter 11 in *Mission in Context: Explorations Inspired by J. Andrew Kirk*, ed. John Corrie and Cathy Ross (Aldershot, UK: Ashgate, 2012), and Andrew F. Walls, *Crossing Cultural Frontiers: Studies in the History of World Christianity* (Maryknoll, NY: Orbis Books, 2017), chapter 3.

Chapter 6

"Monks and Evangelicals" is from *The Birth of the Missionary Movement*, 18–19, original lecture transcripts from OMSC, also published in slightly revised form in Andrew Walls, *The*

Missionary Movement from the West: A Biography from Birth to Old Age, ed. Brian Stanley (Grand Rapids: Eerdmans, 2023), 20–22, 30. Reprinted by permission of the publisher.

Chapter 7

Portions previously published as "World Christianity and the Early Church," in *A New Day: Essays on World Christianity in Honor of Lamin Sanneh*, ed. Akintunde E. Akinade (New York: Peter Lang, 2010), 17–30; and as "The Break-up of Early World Christianity and the Great Ecumenical Failure," *Studies in World Christianity* 28:2 (2022): 156–168.

Chapter 8

"Conversion and Christian Continuity," *Mission Focus* 18, no. 2 (June 1980): 17–21.

Index

P'Bitek, Okot, 88
Persian Empire, 99, 103, 107–8
Peru, 61, 63
Peter (apostle), 17, 23
phenomenal world, 32, 75, 89
Philip, John, 69
Philippines, 61, 64
Pietism, 4, 95–97
Plato, 27–28, 92
pleroma, 32
popular religion, 24–25
Portugal, 60–61, 64–65, 67
praxis, ix–x
proselyte model, 17, 19, 21
Protestantism
   Enlightenment, 83
   missionary movement, 5, 68, 87
   Reformation, 57, 59–60, 83,
      95, 124
   on revelation, 83
   on salvation, 4
Puritans, 4, 95–96

Quechua, 62

Ragnarok, 45
Reformation, 57, 59–60, 83, 95,
   124
resurrection, 28, 48–49, 92
revelation, 13, 83–85
Righteous Remnant, 95
Roman culture
   and barbarians, 38
   and early church, 40, 58, 104–5,
      111–12
   kinship groups, 58
   law, 33, 37, 52, 104

and paganism, 104
and popular religion, 25
Roman Empire
   in Africa, 106–7, 110
   and barbarians, 38, 105
   Council of Chalcedon, 112
   and early church, 29, 37, 42,
      58, 99, 103–4
   and popular religion, 25
   Western, 38–39, 111, 121
Rufinus, Tyrannius, 106
Ruth the Moabitess, 15–16

Sadducees, 14
Sahidic, 99, 106
salvation
   approaches to, 4
   and colonial missionaries, 62, 69
   and Enlightenment, 84
   and Israel, 10–12, 118–19
   and Protestantism, 4
Samaria, 21
Samaritans, 13–14
Samarkand, 109
Sanneh, Lamin, 3, 66
Scriptures
   and Chinese culture, 109–10
   and conversion, 6
   and Enlightenment, 86
   and Gothic language, 99, 105
   and Greek thought, 29–34
   on Messianism, 16
Second World War. *See* World
   War II
secularization, 61, 84, 123
Sepúlveda, Juan Ginés de, 63
Shakers, xii